Simulations in Language Teaching

NEW DIRECTIONS IN LANGUAGE TEACHING
Editors: Howard B. Altman and Peter Strevens

This important new series is for language teachers and others who:
– need to be informed about the key issues facing the language teaching profession today;
– want to understand the theoretical issues underlying current debates;
– wish to relate theory to classroom practice.

In this series:
Communicative Language Teaching: an introduction by William Littlewood
Developing Reading Skills: A practical guide to reading comprehension exercises by Françoise Grellet
Simulations in Language Teaching by Ken Jones

Simulations in Language Teaching

Ken Jones

Cambridge University Press

Cambridge
London   New York   New Rochelle
Melbourne   Sydney

Published by the Press Syndicate of the University of Cambridge
The Pitt Building, Trumpington Street, Cambridge CB2 1RP
32 East 57th Street, New York, NY 10022, USA
296 Beaconsfield Parade, Middle Park, Melbourne 3206, Australia

© Cambridge University Press 1982

First published 1982

Printed at the University Press, Cambridge

Library of Congress catalogue card number: 82–4557

British Library cataloguing in publication data

Jones, Ken
Simulations in language teaching – (New directions in language teaching)
1. Language, Modern – Study and teaching
I. Title   II. Series
418′.007′8   PB49
ISBN 0 521 24885 X hardcovers
ISBN 0 521 27045 6 paperback

2 09895

MU

Contents

Contents

Selected points for skip readers

1 For a brief account of what a simulation is, and also what it is not, turn to 'A simulation defined' in Chapter 1.

2 For guidance in choosing simulations which have the right sort of language level for your students, and how to fit them into the syllabus, read the first two sections in Chapter 2.

3 If you are not sure whether a simulation needs to be altered before being used with your students, then read 'Adapting' in Chapter 3, and also Chapter 6 – 'Will the simulation work?'

4 If you are wondering what sort of discourse can occur in a simulation and how it can be analysed, then read 'Analysing simulation discourse' and 'Whatever happened to Erid?' in Chapter 5.

5 A very brief history of the development of the simulation technique for assessing language and behaviour is given in 'Spies, managers and civil servants' and 'Simulations in language examinations' in Chapter 7.

6 If you want to study the documents of a complete simulation with permission to photocopy it and try it out with friends and colleagues, then turn to Appendix A – *We're not going to use simulations.*

7 Should you want instant reminders of key points you have read in this book, then turn to Appendix B.

Introduction

The simulation technique is a recent innovation in language teaching. Yet it is rapidly increasing in popularity because it is ideally suited to language practice.

A simulation is an event. It is not taught. The students become participants and shape the event. They have roles, functions, duties and responsibilities – as ecologist, king, manager, explorer, reporter, survivor, administrator – within a structured situation involving problem solving and decision making.

The teacher, as Controller, introduces the simulation and is in charge of the mechanics of who is who, and who sits where. But the Controller does not interfere with the decision making and is thus in an excellent position to monitor the language, behaviour and communication skills of the participants.

In a simulation there is reality of function, not pretence. The chairman in a simulation really is a chairman, with the full powers and responsibilities of chairmanship. This reality is often augmented by the realistic nature of the simulated documents and materials, when letters and memos, treaties and balance sheets are reproduced to look like the genuine article.

This book is intended to be a practical guide to language teachers who are thinking of using simulations for the first time, or who are seeking ways of improving their use of the method. The book distinguishes between simulations and other techniques – games, exercises and informal drama – as it is important for the teacher to get the words and concepts right, otherwise the wrong behaviour is likely to follow. There is a nitty-gritty examination of the potential benefits of simulations in language teaching, and there is advice on how to pick a good simulation, how to introduce and run a simulation, and on the follow-up. There is a section, which is important for practical and theoretical reasons, on the analysis of simulation discourse.

The potentialities for using simulations for language assessment are also examined closely, with examples of behavioural assessment both inside and outside the educational field. The author suggests that examination boards, course designers, tutors and teachers should ask the question 'Can simulations help assessment?'

To help the teacher explain aspects of the simulation technique to students, colleagues, administrators and parents, there are lists of Key Reminders for instant reference. And in Appendix A there is a complete set of simulation materials by the author, which can be photocopied and used with any group of colleagues or friends. It is *We're not going to use simulations*, a simulation about the simulation technique in language teaching, which won an award in the English Speaking Union's English Language Competition (1981).

The book's conclusion is that there is no substitute for simulations in language teaching. No other classroom technique provides the same blend of reality and responsibility within a language context. But because simulations are unique, they offer no threat to the textbook, the discussion, the language laboratory, or the teacher. They complement other techniques, and provide a practice ground and an assessment tool.

The use of the simulation technique is one expression of the philosophy that students should be active participants in the learning process.

1 Why use simulations?

A simulation defined

The trouble with the dictionary definition of 'simulation' is that it is a signpost pointing in the wrong direction. It points towards artificiality, pretence, feigning, mimicry and informal drama or even games, with 'substitute elements', 'representations' and so on.

The first step must be to turn the signpost round so that it points towards what actually happens in a simulation. This can be done by looking at the essential elements, and then defining the word 'simulation' accordingly. Experience suggests that all simulations must contain three essential elements:

REALITY OF FUNCTION

This covers not only what the participants say and do, but also what they think. They must mentally accept the function the simulation requires of them. They must stop thinking of themselves as students, and avoid standing one step away from their own activities. They must step inside the function mentally and behaviourally, and do the best they can to carry out their duties and responsibilities in the situation in which they find themselves.

Acceptance of the reality of function means that the participant who has the function of statesman must take decisions in the interests of his country, the reporter who is interviewing him must ask questions conscientiously, and the secretary, the protester, the soldier or the farmer must all strive to communicate effectively.

This automatically rules out play-acting, or playing games, or playing about, or playing the fool, or playing to please (or provoke) the teacher. There is no play − either in a theatrical or in a gaming sense − in a simulation, and if there were, then it would stop being a simulation. Similarly, reality of function excludes the Controller from the problem-solving and decision-making areas. The Controller is not a teacher in a simulation activity; there is no teacher in the cabinet office, the news room, or on the shop floor.

SIMULATED ENVIRONMENT

The environment must be simulated, otherwise it is not a simulation. A learner driver under instruction on the roads, or a student teacher involved in classroom practice, or a medical probationer examining patients are not in a simulated environment. There is real traffic, real pupils, real patients — and real interaction. In order to fulfil the essential condition of being a simulated environment, there must be no contact, interaction or consequences between the participants and the world outside the classroom. In this respect, a simulation is safe; the outside world remains untouched, and real disasters cannot result from participant errors. So, although the functions of the participants are real, the world outside the classroom is, paradoxically, imaginary.

STRUCTURE

A simulation requires a structure. It must be a structure built around some problem or problems, and the structure must be sufficiently explicit to preserve reality of function. The essential 'facts' of the simulation must be provided, and not invented, by the participants. If a teacher says 'Pretend you are journalists on a newspaper and invent your own news items and write your own front page', then this is not a simulation, since there is no reality of function. The participants would be authors, not journalists. There is no structure in this situation; what is needed is news agency material, or reporters' stories, plus an adequate description of the size of the front page, perhaps with an indication of the paper's normal layout, plus a deadline. The cohesion of structure means that a simulation is more involved and involving than a single transactional episode — such as a shopper returning a broken teapot, or a traveller asking for the time of the next train. In practice, a simulation can be thought of as a case study, but with the participants on the inside, having the power and responsibility to shape the event and tackle the problem.

The three elements which are essential to a simulation can be combined into a one-sentence definition:

> A simulation is reality of function in a simulated and structured environment.

Unlike most definitions of simulations, this stresses the reality of the activity and contrasts it with the simulated world outside, and the reference to structure is a guide to distinguishing between simulations and role play. If, of course, the role play involves reality of function, and the environment is simulated adequately and is structured around a problem, then that is a simulation by definition and in practice, and is indistinguishable in kind from the other simulations described in this book.

The definition is broad enough to embrace a wide variety of simulations: long simulations lasting weeks or months, and short simulations lasting no more than half an hour; complicated simulations and simple ones; simulations which have a right answer, and open-ended simulations in which there is no 'right' answer, and the outcome is a matter of opinion and value judgement.

Probably no succinct definition of complex activities can be adequate, and the teacher can regard the definition as little more than a reminder of points of difference between simulations and other related activities — role play, informal drama, exercises, case studies and games. By itself, the definition will not classify borderline cases — that depends on what actually went on during the event, how people behaved and how people thought. For example, some writers classify in-tray exercises as simulations, while others exclude them. An in-tray exercise is an event with only one participant. It is non-interactive. The problem is to deal with the items in the in-tray: a headmaster's in-tray, a manager's in-tray, a clerk's in-tray. This has similar characteristics to a pilot in a flight simulator, except that the electronic equipment provides feedback to the pilot whereas an in-tray exercise usually consists of once-only decision making. However, some in-tray exercises do provide for documents to be fed into the in-tray in response to earlier decisions.

Instead of trying to place all such activities in one pigeon hole, it is more enlightening to ask questions: is it a function which is normally done by one person? Is the participant thinking about the problem in terms of duties and responsibilities, or is he merely operating in a detached way? Has the activity a cohesive structure? Is there sufficient information in the documents or the equipment to preserve reality of function?

As will be seen later in the book, it is useful to accept a category of non-interactive simulations for those solitary activities which fulfil the conditions in the definition.

In the above definition, a simulation is the event, the action. But there are two other fairly common usages which are worth noting. One is to refer to a simulation as comprising not only the action, but also the briefing and the debriefing. This covers the Controller's explanation of the mechanics of the simulation action before it starts, and the final discussion of what happened and what lessons can be drawn from the event. In this sense, a simulation is a three-part event. The second common usage is to apply the word simulation to the materials. Used in this way, it can be said that an author wrote a simulation, a teacher bought a simulation, and simulations are kept in the resource centre. Although strictly speaking this usage is incorrect, it rarely causes confusion since it is clear from the context that the speaker is referring to the documents which comprise the structure of the simulation, not the event itself. It is comparable to the word 'play': 'He wrote a play' and 'She bought a play' refer only to the words on paper; but 'He acted in a play' and 'She saw the play' refer to performance, not paper.

Even though the double usage of 'simulation' to mean documents and action is justifiable, it should not be forgotten that the essence of a simulation is action. A simulation cannot be evaluated merely by reading the materials. It is not self-contained, like a text book. It has to occur, and what occurs may be different from what might be imagined by merely reading the documents. The best part of the simulation is usually a question mark, and the answer is left out of the documents, but is supplied in the action. Authors often insert hidden spurs to action, and concealed curbs to prevent loss of functional reality. Even to observe a simulation in action is not the same as to participate in it. Seeing someone else in the hot seat is a different experience to sitting in it oneself. In a very real sense, a simulation is like a strawberry. It has to be tasted to be appreciated.

Language

Simulations and language are virtually inseparable. Almost all simulations involve a substantial amount of interaction between the participants, and interaction involves language – the spoken word, the written word, or both.

Language in a simulation tends to have two dominant characteristics – it is *cohesive* and *functional*.

It is *cohesive* because of the structure of the simulation. Even though two participants, or two groups of participants, may start the simulation with opposing views, the action brings them together. They concentrate on the issues. They have a built-in motive to analyse, discuss, argue, report, state a case, question, negotiate, conciliate, mediate, explain, denounce, agree, tackle problems and make decisions in a cohesive manner. An example of how this cohesion works in practice can be seen in the section 'Analysing simulation discourse' in Chapter 5. Although a great many explanations and ideas are thrown into the discussion by the participants, they are all relevant to the central problem – how to survive – and are discussed in the light of the criteria of survival. To an outside observer, the language used in a discussion-type simulation may appear little different from that used in a classroom discussion on a particular topic. The difference is that the language is held together by mutual need arising out of the structure of the simulation, the functions of the participants, and the motivation to communicate. In an ordinary classroom discussion a student can say 'That reminds me of...' or 'When I was in Patagonia...', and the discussion can move off in any random direction which appears interesting. Unless it is held together by the teacher, it can finish up a long way from the starting point. So, although some classroom discussions are cohesive in practice, simulations are cohesive because of their nature.

The second dominant characteristic of simulation discourse is that the language is *functional*. The participants have jobs to do, duties to fulfil, and problems to solve. In interactive simulations this means the language of discourse, transaction, negotiation, explanation and inquiry. The word 'function' is not used here in the utilitarian sense of being able to order a meal or ask the way to the beach. It includes all the social language appropriate to the job. If the participant is a diplomat, then the appropriate language is the language of diplomacy, and the appropriate behaviour includes all those social skills and social remarks which can make the diplomacy more effective. If the participant is a judge, then the appropriate functional and social language will be judicial. If the participant is a conservationist protesting against pollution, then the functional language will be the language of protest. A barrister will use the language of advocacy, the coroner will use the language of inquest, the dictator will use the language of power. In a simulation it is up to the participants to suit the language to the occasion. And since most simulations have plenty of opportunities for action, interaction, reaction and counteraction, inappropriate language by one participant can be dealt with in an appropriate way by the other participants. Feedback can be instantaneous.

So in a simulation the language is, by nature, both cohesive and functional. It is the language of action and interaction, the language of fulfilling duties and accepting responsibilities, the language of exploring problems and reaching decisions, all within a structured environment. Used in the above sense, language is not merely the sum total of grammatically acceptable sentences. It is not a matter – to use a Chomsky analogy – of cataloguing words like butterflies on a tray. So, when assessing the value of simulations for the development of language, it is important to examine behaviour, context, motive, meaning and shared knowledge. What goes on in the minds of the participants is relevant to the Controller's assessment. A sentence can be grammatically correct, yet functionally inadequate and unsuitable. Similarly, some sentences can communicate highly effectively, even though they contain some grammatical inaccuracies.

From this description of functional and cohesive language it can be seen that simulations fit in well with the 'communicative' movement that developed in the 1970s and changed the direction of a great deal of language teaching. As Littlewood (1981) put it:

> The learner must distinguish between the forms which he has mastered as part of his linguistic competence, and the communicative functions that they perform. In other words, items mastered as part of a *linguistic* system must also be understood as part of a *communicative* system.
> The learner must develop skills and strategies for using language to communicate meanings as effectively as possible in concrete situations. He must learn to use feedback to judge his success, and if necessary, remedy failure by using different language.

The variety of functions and situations available in simulations provides rich opportunities for language skills. The briefing has the language of explanation; the action has the language of functional interaction; and the debriefing has the language of inquest.

Communication skills

Although communication is not the same as language, the two are closely dependent. To emphasise communication skills is to emphasise language in use, not for its own sake, but to achieve a functional purpose. Simulations provide the participants with the mutual need to communicate. The need is inherent in the activity; it is not a teacher-directed need. The participants do not communicate in order to please the Controller, or in order to learn language skills, but because of the duties inherent in their functions. Compared with a typical classroom discussion, the communication skills used in simulations are far more varied. They range from the informal chat about a problem to making a speech at the (simulated) United Nations Assembly. The communication skills can involve journalism, advertising, diplomacy, negotiations, oratory, chairmanship, analysis, politics, economics and so on.

Once set in motion by the Controller, a good simulation is like a nuclear power breeder reactor; it produces its own fuel. Communication leads to more communication, ideas generate ideas, talk leads to thought, and thought leads to talk. A note from the Prime Minister of Blueland to the President of Redland can generate an informal meeting, a summit conference, a treaty, a day of prayer, or mobilisation of the army. Not only does talk generate thought within the simulation, but a good deal of the learning may occur afterwards, through reflection and discussion. Participants remember vividly what they tried to communicate, how they tried to do it, and what happened as a result. The vividness of such memories is highly beneficial for language learning.

Communication in a simulation does not have to be successful to be beneficial. Failures are as desirable as successes. Simulations are not drills or programmed learning. If, after a simulation, the teacher says 'That simulation did not work well because the participants failed to find the most suitable answer', then this is a mistake of category; the teacher is confusing the simulation technique with other methods. In simulations generally, questions are more important than answers, and learning is more important than 'success'.

In a simulation, the communication is not always related solely to the subject matter. Very often the participants have to organise themselves in order to tackle a problem efficiently. They may have to work out their priorities – which aspect to tackle first – and produce their own agenda. They may elect a leader or spokesman, or divide the labour among themselves, or work out their own procedures. These organisational activities require communication skills. With advanced students who are familiar with simulations, the teacher may decide to give the job of Controller to one or two of the students, thus adding further variety to the organisational and communication skills practised by the students. Even if the Controller remains firmly in charge of the action, the organisational job of introducing the simulation and chairing the subsequent follow-up discussion might be allocated to a student; or, in the

9

case of a large simulation, to a committee of students. The communicative abilities related to organisational skills have a high level of transferability. In fact, one of the reasons why communication skills are so valuable a factor in simulations is their transfer value. It is not only the skill itself that is transferred, but also the confidence and initiative which accompany it.

Skills at communicating news items in a media simulation are not restricted to the field of journalism; many people on many occasions find the need to select and communicate news items, of one sort or another. The skills of statesmen in an international affairs simulation find ready transference to the world outside the classroom; diplomacy is also useful at home, at work and on holiday. And so on.

Most people are not very good at dealing with the unfamiliar event, and experience in simulations can help to develop the ability to think and communicate in an unfamiliar situation. A simulation related to futurology, for example, may have little value as a vehicle for learning facts, but a high value in transferable organisational and communicative skills.

Generally speaking, the language teacher is in the favourable position of not being particularly restricted by the subject matter of a simulation. Providing the simulation is well designed, fully participative, and has plenty of opportunities for communication, then it may not matter too much whether the subject is geography, ecology, business, or journalism. To place language and communication skills as the first criterion of choice is to open the door to a great many well-tested and fascinating simulations.

Motivation

Of all the reasons for using simulations in language teaching, motivation is one of the most important, and is probably the most interesting.

Motivation is inherent in a simulation. It is an integral part. It is not something that is added on by the students; it is part of the structure of the simulation. Motive arises out of the function, the duties, the responsibilities and the circumstances in which the participants find themselves. It is self-generated and usually grows and develops as the interaction develops. It feeds upon itself, strengthening and reinforcing behaviour and language. In this sense, motivation is not a matter of 'getting the students interested'. It depends only on the participants accepting the reality of their functions. If participants accept their function and conscientiously try to do their best, then motivation is inevitable.

The strength of the motivation depends on the simulation (is it a good, well-designed simulation or a poor one?) and on its suitability for the particular students, and on whether the teacher's briefing has been adequate and satisfactory. This sort of motivation is quite different from that of students who perform a classroom task in order to complete the course, pass the examination, please the teacher, or even please themselves. Suppose, for example, that in a committee simulation a participant jots down notes of those points on which he is in agreement or disagreement with other committee members. The motivation is not to please the teacher or himself, or in order to learn language or communication skills. There is no question of the participant thinking 'Do I have to do this writing?' The activity is voluntary and spontaneous. The motivation is empirical. The aim is entirely practical, relating to functional efficiency.

In this, and a thousand other examples, the motive is inherent in the circumstances of the event, and it applies to all forms of behaviour. The participant may be thinking, writing, speaking, stating a case, interviewing, listening, organising, debating, and yet the motivation for these actions is the same: acceptance of the duties and the desire to function effectively.

Motivation from function and duty is an essential ingredient in a simulation. It would not, by definition, be a simulation if this motivation were absent. But it is not the only type of motivation experienced by the participants. If the simulation is well designed, fully participative, stimulating and provocative, then there is likely to be a large measure of emotional satisfaction, which can have a strong motivational effect. Some authors refer to it as 'fun', but this is not a good description. More appropriate words might be 'enjoyment', 'pleasure' or 'satisfaction'. It includes the emotional satisfaction of a job well done (or interestingly done), the pleasures of power, the self-esteem of responsible decision making, and the delight of interactive excitement. Participants 'own' the simulation; and there is pride in ownership. This double motivation, from within the action and because of it, can result in experiences of high quality, which can be remembered very clearly weeks, months and even years after the event.

The functional nature of the motivation affects different people differently, depending on their personalities. The behaviour of an extrovert in a simulation may be little different from his normal behaviour. But the introverts, the shy and the self-conscious students often find simulations are a form of behavioural therapy. Duty begets bravery; responsibility results in action, communication and language. After a simulation it is not uncommon for the teacher to say, or think, 'I was amazed at the behaviour of students A and B. They did really well. I never thought they could do that.' And this amazement is often not restricted to the teacher; it can surprise the students themselves, who had undervalued their own abilities, and can be a talking point afterwards in the coffee shops.

One of the main reasons why teachers of foreign languages find simulations so useful is that they destroy the teacher–student orientation, and kick the teacher out of the classroom. Inhibitions and fears tend to diminish and may vanish altogether because the participants are talking to each other, not to the teacher. And their talk is not casual chat, but related to duties.

The confidence gained through simulations is also based on practice. It is not the 'I've read it, so now I know it' type of confidence. It is the 'I've done it, so I can do it' confidence. It is based on the experience of success, not merely the expectation of success.

Shyness is not the only barrier which can be broken down through the motivation of simulations. Random allocation of functions and roles breaks up cliques, and brings together students who otherwise would say little to each other. The motivation can overcome the differences of race, colour, sex, creed and status. It shakes up the pecking order in a class. Motivation in a simulation tends to equalise power, and equalise opportunities, and can thus produce some surprising results.

From the point of view of educational psychology and learning theory, the motivation arising from simulations provides a fruitful source of study. And certainly from the viewpoint of the practising language teacher, the motivation in a good simulation has considerable and diverse benefits.

Icebreaking

A simulation is an event which helps students get to know one another, and helps the teacher get to know the students. So quite apart from its other values, it can be used, and often is used, as an icebreaker at the beginning of a course or at the commencement of a new school year. A good simulation can break up the frosty silences, allow and encourage well-motivated talk and action, and provide an interesting experience, which has important social aspects. Even if it is a confrontational type of simulation involving two or more groups, friendships can develop across group boundaries as well as within groups. Perhaps this is partly because everyone is in the same simulation; a fellow feeling develops, a sort of participants' club. As mentioned earlier, simulations can result in memorable experiences, which can bring students together outside the classroom, as well as inside it. The classroom door may close at the end of the simulation, but the talk can continue.

Icebreaking can occur whenever ice has formed; it need not be restricted to beginnings. For a variety of reasons a class may solidify into undesirable routine. Students might continually sit in the same chairs, mix with the same groups, and develop their own routine reactions to the teacher. And, of course, teachers can also get into ruts.

In some language classes, ethnic groups tend to coalesce, and this may occur later in the course rather than earlier. Groups can coalesce according to their sex, status, or even ability. Sometimes the groups can be regarded as friendship groups, sometimes as cliques, cabals, or even gangs. The view of the group from inside might be very different from how it is seen by those outside it. By its nature, group behaviour not only tends to cement attitudes within the group, but also, if only by its existence, creates suspicion and perhaps hostility from those outside the group.

If such groups appear to hinder rather than help the educational process, then the teacher is faced with a professional problem. If class time is taken up with incidents caused by inter-group rivalry, accompanied by unco-operative or even disruptive behaviour, then the problem can hardly be ignored. In such circumstances, simulations offer a possible solution. One advantage is that the ice can be broken by indirect means, thus avoiding the teacher clashing head-on with group loyalties. Not only is it an indirect attempt at a solution, but it is also a positive one, since simulations emphasise and encourage ice-breaking behaviour patterns.

If the ice is what might be called 'group ice', as distinct from 'individual ice', then the teacher might be faced with a problem if the students ask or demand to remain in their groups in the simulation. There are several ways to get round this. One is for the teacher to insist on the professional reasons for random allocation of roles – that for language and communicative purposes it is educationally desirable that students should have an opportunity of trying to work with people who are not their close friends, since in the outside world it is often very necessary to co-operate with all sorts of people. Another way is to choose a simulation which has no groups. A third way is to pick a simulation in which groups split up and re-form into new groups during the various stages of the simulation.

Obviously, not all simulations are suitable icebreakers. Some simulations are non-interactive, and thus break no ice. Others involve a high proportion of written work, are highly subject-orientated, and contain little interaction. Other simulations could be ruled out because they are too long, too complicated, too difficult, or even too simple and too easy.

Likely candidates for the job of icebreaking are those simulations which are fully participatory, having no passive or part-time roles or functions, which are reasonably short, which involve plenty of interaction and movement among participants and groups, and which are interesting, stimulating and even exciting.

Realism

The language teacher and the language student are continuously aware of the need to apply the learning of the language to the world outside the classroom. Whereas the student of geography or history can regard the acquisition of knowledge and skills as a long-term investment, the learning of languages can usually be tested in the here and now. Foreign broadcasts, foreign books and newspapers, and foreigners themselves are usually available both inside and outside the teaching institution. This need for reality makes it easy for the language teacher to sell the idea of simulations to students, colleagues, administrators and parents.

As emphasised earlier, the reality of the function is an essential and inescapable part of the simulation experience. And it is difficult to appreciate this point fully unless one has had this experience.

A consequence of this reality is that participants often become oblivious to anything that is not directly relevant to the simulation experience. The Controller becomes invisible; the walls and classroom notices vanish from consciousness; the routine sights and sounds of the classroom and the building disappear from the mind. This relates to the point made in defining a simulation – that what goes on in the minds of the participants is part of the event. And if the minds are focussed on the other participants, the functions and the problems, then the event has a very high degree of realism. It explains why many participants, having experienced a simulation for the first time, say things like 'That was real. That was real life.' To some extent, of course, it may be realism that they have never previously experienced, and never will experience in the outside world. They may never have the experience of chairing a committee or deciding how many articles to manufacture, or negotiating with a foreign power. It might not be too strong to suggest that it is not only realism, but a kind of magical realism – a world which grants the secret wish for power and prestige, respect and self-esteem.

It is useful for the teacher to think of realism as including the thoughts of the participants, as this helps to correct a fairly common tendency to think of realism only in terms of the contents of the simulation's structure. Teachers, and others, sometimes look at the materials in the simulation pack and complain that it is incomplete and unrealistic. If it is a local simulation, they say it should give details of how the location fits into the national picture. If it is a national simulation, they ask for the international details. If it is international, then they ask for more details about the history – political, social and economic – of each country, together with the international treaties and the rules and conventions of the United Nations.

This is a pre-Raphaelite view of simulations – the well-meaning but erroneous desire to paint in every leaf of the tree in the name of realism. At one time, simulation designers tried to provide such realism, with huge scenarios giving detail upon detail of organisations and institutions, historical and descriptive, which were involved in, or peripheral to, the action. And this fitted in with a fact-learning approach to the simulation technique, which was more common in the 1950s and 1960s than it is today.

For most simulation designers these days, realism does not mean lots of realistic details; they are more concerned with the realism of function and the realism of the essential aspects of a situation. This historical development of simulations favours today's language teacher, since it produces a great many highly interesting, action-filled simulations; and they are not cluttered up with sophisticated detail, which can daunt the language student.

Because realism is painted on a broad canvas, it means that the door is open for simulations located in the future, in outer space, in prehistory, all of which can produce highly realistic communication, problem solving and decision making, with the additional advantage of shaking up any stultified thought patterns.

Another historical development which benefits language teaching is the move into realism in simulation documents. At one time they were either incorporated into an overall general description, and were not separate documents at all, or else they were separate, but produced without realism. Nowadays, a handwritten letter usually looks like a handwritten letter; an advertising brochure is given the style and artwork of the real article, and a dull invoice is made to look like a dull invoice.

Such realism helps the teacher to sell the simulation idea to students, course designers and parents as being language orientated. And once a simulation has been used in the class, the teacher can reintroduce any of the documents in subsequent lessons, since they are already familiar: 'You may remember in the media simulation that the journalists received this handout – do you think this was information or advertising?'

Cross-cultural simulations

As already seen, simulations in general can help to break down cultural and ethnic prejudices. By their nature they are non-discriminatory, particularly as a random allocation of functions and roles ensures fair play. They involve everyone working to a purpose, with equality of power and opportunity within the function and structure of the event. No one has to defer to anyone else because of their status in the class, or in a group, or because of their sex.

This section, however, is concerned solely with that small but influential group of simulations which deliberately introduce cultural and ethnical differences for educational and social purposes. They all have roughly the same aim, to help understanding and communication between cultures, but the structure and content vary considerably. In some simulations the cultural differences are reinforced by economic differences: the haves and have-nots. Some simulations specify the race: blacks, whites, and so on. Others take a more general and indirect approach – with groups representing friends or strangers, insiders or outsiders, the native population or the immigrants, the visitors or the visited.

Some of these simulations, such as Garry Shirts' *Bafá Bafá*, use completely fictitious cultures – the Alpha culture and the Beta culture – which not only serves as a prototype of cultural understanding and misunderstanding, but also helps to avoid accusations that the cross-cultural simulations themselves have some devious racist aim.

Cross-cultural simulations tend to arouse controversy for several reasons. Firstly there are the misunderstandings of those who are not involved in the activity. Secondly there are the emotions and prejudices which can be revealed during the simulation itself, and thirdly there may be controversy over whether the simulation is a fair representation of ethnic problems outside the classroom. On this last point, it is important to be sure that the simulation really is a simulation, and not a pre-programmed exercise in confrontation. If participants are told to play-act emotions which may not be their normal reactions in such situations, then the reality of function is diminished or destroyed. In such circumstances the participants may well feel aggrieved at being manipulated. In a genuine simulation the participants must have the power to function as best they can according to the circumstances. If that power is diminished because the role card says they are angry, frightened, apathetic, bad-tempered, insensitive, impulsive, dogmatic, compromising, good-natured, indecisive and so on, then the resultant activity is not a simulation. If, on the other hand, the emotions, judgements, decisions, communications and thoughts of the participants arise solely out of the nature of the situation – even though the situation may be untypical – then that would still be a simulation. It is one thing to be at the mercy of events; it is quite a different thing to have a personality transplant.

Leaving aside non-simulations, there is still a wide range of emotional involvement which varies from simulation to simulation, and from participant to participant. At one extreme the problem is almost entirely intellectual and observational. A participant might think: 'Members of that culture keep looking at the floor when they talk to us. How should I interpret that behaviour? Does it mean that they are shy, shifty or ashamed, or is the eyes-down behaviour an expression of politeness and non-aggression?' A participant in the other group might think: 'Those people keep staring at us when they speak. Why is that? Are they deliberately being rude, hostile or impolite, or is it their way of showing frankness, openness and friendship?' The actual behaviour patterns may be necessary as part of the structure of the simulation and inherent in the briefing of the individual groups, but the interpretation of such behaviour is up to the participants themselves. They observe what they observe, and it is in their power to behave according to their interpretation of what is going on.

The interesting, and self-revealing aspect, is that while such a simulation may begin on a note of impartiality and good nature, the emotional 'We're doing the right thing so they must be at fault' attitude may soon start to form in the minds of some, or all, of the participants.

At the other extreme is a simulation which starts with a history of conflict. It may be part of the background information that strong grievances exist, and they have to be taken into account. Some participants, either when the simulation starts, or during its development, may feel that their status is unfairly prejudiced by laws, customs, or the behaviour of the other group or groups. One group may start the simulation with high-value artifacts – houses, factories, gold – while the other group may have much lower-value artifacts. It is not unusual for inequalities to be built into such simulations. But whether those involved react with tolerance or intolerance must be a matter for the participants. The behaviour must not be pre-empted and predetermined by the role cards. Simulations involve people, not stereotypes.

If an alleged simulation is half functional and half play-acting, then an unpleasant or unsatisfactory mishmash can occur. In the debriefing the Controller might ask a participant, 'Why did you spend your time looking out of the window?' 'Because my role card said I felt pretty apathetic about the situation.' 'But you are supposed to participate in a simulation.' 'I was participating by proving just how apathetic I was.' But because a cross-cultural simulation involves the genuine thoughts and behaviour of the participants, that is no guarantee that explosions will not occur, either in the action or in the debriefing. Arguments may become long and heated precisely because the emotions and attitudes are genuine. It not infrequently happens that people who hold humanitarian and tolerant views in theory and in public, may reveal to themselves and perhaps the other participants that they behave differently when it comes to the crunch. Such self-contradictions can arouse a variety of emotional behaviour – honest confession, guilty silence, or aggressive justification.

For these reasons, the debriefing is extremely important. It might be the most valuable part of the activity. Time must be allowed to let people have their say, and to give the Controller an opportunity to defuse what might be an explosive situation, by turning the attention to parallel situations, and trying to draw lessons from the experiences. If the debriefing is perfunctory, then there is the danger of reinforcing or exacerbating cultural prejudices, not to mention personal prejudices. Consequently, the teacher who wishes to use a cross-cultural simulation should be certain to try it out first with some colleagues in order to assess its volatility, and should not introduce it unless confident of handling any subsequent emotional outbursts.

Nevertheless, it is a fact that many language teachers are drawn towards cross-cultural simulations, and have used them successfully. Sometimes this draws them into the wider field of simulation usage. Certainly, there is an affinity between the struggle to overcome language barriers, and overcoming barriers which are ethnic, religious, social and cultural.

Monitoring

Simulations provide teachers with a unique opportunity to monitor, assess and appreciate the participants, not just for their language abilities as students, but as whole people. No other classroom activity provides more invisibility for the teacher. The high level of motivation in a good, well-run simulation is as effective as a naturalist's hide. Providing the Controller is not deliberately intrusive, monitoring has no problems and many benefits.

One benefit is that the teacher has virtually nothing to do but monitor. Assuming that the preparatory work has been done adequately, and the participants are clear about the procedures, then the physical functions of the Controller are likely to be those of a low-grade clerk – handing out documents at the right time, and so on. This leaves plenty of time and opportunity to monitor the language, the communication skills, and the social interchanges that characterise interactive simulations.

At first, the function of Controller may not be particularly easy if the teacher is used to intervening to help the students. There may be an initial feeling of guilt that it is too easy, and too enjoyable. But after a little practice, the teacher will soon find that it is a justifiable activity, not least because it educates the teacher. As Controller, the teachers learn a great deal that otherwise would not be observable, from the points of view of language, skills, behaviour and character.

As will be discussed in detail later, the monitoring need not be restricted to the particular simulation and the particular language used in the activity. It can be regarded as part of long-term classroom assessment – taking notes of general strengths and weaknesses of particular students, noting improvements of techniques and confidence, and using such observations at appropriate moments during the course. Since simulations are language in action, they reveal what really has been learned at a practical level, as distinct from things the students thought they knew, but did not, or were unable to use in communication outside the graded exercises or question-and-answer sessions with the teacher.

Apart from the positive side of monitoring, there are the negative benefits for the Controller, which include not being constantly on tap for answers, and not diligently guiding the students along a pre-planned path. The Controller can relax and this probably increases the value of the monitoring activities. Goodbye teacher, and welcome Controller, can be liberating, invigorating, entertaining and informative.

2 Choosing simulations for the language classroom

Matching the language level

Choosing simulations to match the language level of the students is an important problem, but one which rapidly diminishes in difficulty as the teacher gains experience in simulation use.

Participation is the surest avenue to suitability of choice. The teacher should participate in the simulation before presenting it to the students. This need not be a full-scale affair. Corners can be cut, roles reduced, and the action truncated, providing that the resultant activities give a good idea of what sort of language level is desirable, and also of the minimum language ability required.

Trial runs can be organised with any convenient guinea pigs: colleagues, friends, family, or advanced students. If the teaching is done in a large institution, and if there are half a dozen or more staff who are interested in the simulation technique, then it might be possible to start up an official, or unofficial, guinea pig club.

The need for trial runs is because a simulation is not like a book; it cannot be assessed effectively by reading the materials. It is an event; it requires participation in the experience. But once the teacher becomes familiar with simulations, how they work, and how much and what sort of reading, writing and communications are involved, then matching the simulations to the language level becomes much easier.

If the students as well as the teacher are familiar with simulations, then the matching of the level of the materials to the ability becomes easier still, since the question can be discussed with the students, who will be aware of the functional opportunities entailed in simulations. They will thus be in a good position to know whether the functional level will be too difficult for them.

Experience shows that if the language teacher and the students have no practical experience of simulations, then the teacher's estimate of what the students can achieve in simulations is likely to be too low rather than too high. There are several reasons for this, all of them based on the nature of the simulation technique.

The main reason is that the teacher is likely to underestimate the strength of the motivation which occurs in simulations generally. The participants really want to fulfil their functions. They appreciate being given power and authority. They get wrapped up in the development of events. They strive to discharge their duties. As a consequence of this motivation, the participants help each other in dealing with the situation in which they find themselves. If a participant does not understand an aspect of language, then the other participants willingly help. Apprehension by the teacher that the simulation will result in individual participants floundering about in helpless isolation is to make an error of category. Participants in a simulation are not battery hens in boxes. They are a mutual help society. And the group level of linguistic accomplishment is above the average ability of the individuals comprising the group, since the more able participants tend to lead, explain and advise.

A second reason for underestimating the ability of students to cope with a simulation is to overestimate the nature of the task, and to think of the objective in terms of accuracy rather than of opportunity. Simulations come into the phase of learning which Littlewood (1981) described as 'learner directed communicative activities'. As he says, the students have to use

> *whatever language they have at their disposal.* That is, they are not required to attempt to choose language which is appropriate to any particular situation. It may not even matter whether the language they use is grammatically accurate. The main purpose of the activity is that learners should use the language they know in order to get meanings across as effectively as possible. Success is measured primarily according to whether they cope with the communicative demands of the immediate situation.

In fact, the teacher can consider failure to be an important benefit. People learn from their mistakes. The practice of language in a simulation is an opportunity to get it wrong as well as to get it right.

A third reason for undervaluing the ability of the participants in a particular simulation is a failure to assess the mechanics of the simulation correctly. Just because there are a lot of documents in the simulation pack does not mean that all participants have to read all the documents. Some documents may be confidential to one or two participants only. Others may be there, not for reading and learning, but for reference. It is useful for the teacher, when examining the documents, to say 'If I were participant X, what would I have to do, and who would be able to help me do it?'

The best procedure, as mentioned earlier, is for the teacher to actually participate in the simulation with a group of friends or colleagues. Teacher participation may reveal that the language level of the simulation is entirely suitable, except for one or two specific points. Perhaps one of the documents is overlong, intricate, complicated and too sophisticated. If presented to the participants 'cold', then it could have a daunting effect. They might throw up their hands in despair, or at best spend a lot of time trying to understand the document, and this could unbalance the whole simulation. In these circumstances, the teacher has two choices: either abandon the simulation altogether and look for one which is more suitable, or else adapt the document in order to simplify the language, or perhaps find a more effective way of introducing it than that suggested in the Controller's notes. The techniques of adaptation are described in the next chapter – 'Preparing for the simulation'.

Simulations in the syllabus

In theory, and also in practice, simulations should be allocated whatever share of the syllabus is appropriate to their educational importance in the particular situation. This level of priority can vary with the ability of the students and the aims of the teacher or course designer.

As a general principle, simulations should be given enough time for students to realise their importance, and enough prominence in the outline of the syllabus for students to understand that simulations are a unique educational technique, particularly suited to language learning. And these points could be made in the pre-course publicity. If the students are unfamiliar with simulations, then it could be worthwhile including an introductory half-hour during which the teacher can explain what simulations are, what they are not, and can give examples of the range of opportunities for language practice which simulations contain.

The question of which simulations to fit into the syllabus, and at which stage, depends on matching the resources with the aims. Since there are plenty of simulations available, at least in English, and since simulations are usually fairly flexible in the number of participants and the amount of time required, the most useful first step may be to clarify the aims. The teacher can use a checklist from the section headings in the previous chapter – language, communication skills, motivation, icebreaking, realism, cross-cultural simulations, monitoring – and work out an outline of the main priorities. An important aspect may be the section on monitoring, since this includes assessment of students' ability, and is discussed at greater length in Chapter 7.

If the syllabus is concentrated on a specific subject area – business communications, maritime law and procedures, journalism, social customs and cultures – then this may predetermine the area of choice. Indeed, only one or two published simulations might be available in the subject. Restricted choice can be met by adapting a simulation if it is unsuitable for the language level, or else by widening the area of choice by including an icebreaker from another subject.

It sometimes happens that when the members of a course are already experts or professionals in their own field, they do not want simulations (or exercises, or role play) based on factual data associated with that field; they want to learn how to communicate data. This means that the teacher is not compelled to look up a catalogue of simulations and choose one with a subject-related title. If the group is composed of industrial chemists, they will not attend the language course to learn chemistry, but to learn how to give and receive technical data in the language being studied. So rather than select what might be a dull or over-simplified simulation about chemistry, it would be worthwhile looking at other simulations which involve communications about technical data – from the oil industry, town planning, ecology and so forth – and approach the problem from the point of view of language communication, not fact learning. Experience also suggests that a completely different subject area to that familiar to the experts may be welcomed as a refreshing change, while at the same time providing the service required – practice in language and communication skills, in social awareness, and in sensitivity to cultural differences.

Obviously, the wider the choice of simulations, the more chance there is of finding ones which have the right language level, are well designed, and result in a high level of motivation and interaction. So even if the course is subject orientated, the alternative to restricted choice may be improved publicity and information about simulations for language practice when advertising the course.

Another possible restriction on the choice is to look only in language literature for suitable simulations. There is no reason to suppose that a language teacher can write a more exciting simulation than a geography teacher. Providing the simulation written by the geography teacher has the right sort of language level for the particular students, then it may be superior. There are also the professional authors, who are expert in designing simulations, and who can usually be relied upon to produce simulations which work well in practice, are easy to run, and provoke and excite ideas and communications. To ignore such products on the grounds that the authors are not language experts is to misunderstand the nature of simulations.

Widening simulation choice for meeting the requirements of the syllabus is not a fearsome task of looking at the literature for each subject area in order to find out if someone in that field has designed a simulation which might be suitable. Apart from delving into the professional language magazines and books, the other main field is simulation literature – as outlined later in this chapter, and in the bibliography. Simulation users are continually on the look-out for good simulations which can be used for language across the curriculum, and they are listed and described in simulation literature.

In choosing simulations for the curriculum it is useful to think of them as developing agents. They are not merely isolated educational activities; they often influence their surroundings – students, teacher and syllabus – by throwing up ideas, and imparting motivation and confidence, which can have a beneficial effect generally. So in planning the syllabus it is useful to have some degree of flexibility in the period immediately after a simulation has taken place, in order to be able to take advantage of beneficial side effects. Otherwise, the teacher may have to say 'Sorry, I know you are very keen on this follow-up activity, but we have no time for it in the syllabus.'

Another characteristic of simulations which should be borne in mind is the accelerator effect of having several simulations during the course. If the students are new to simulations, then the first one will take up relatively more time than the second, because students need to get used to the possibilities, and the extent of their power and responsibilities. By the time the second and third simulations have come along, the participants may be helping the Controller to run the simulation, perhaps even taking over the job of Controller. By using several simulations, the anticipation of the event, the event itself, and its repercussions in confidence, ability and initiative, can make it easier for the teacher to cover the normal course work. This accelerator effect also influences the teacher – providing an oasis of relaxed assessment time – and thereby increases the effectiveness of the teacher's judgement of language and communication priorities during the whole of the course.

If it is the sort of course where the teacher's assessment of the students counts towards the formal marks awarded for the course, then whatever techniques the teacher uses become part of the examination procedures. In this case, simulations are therefore in themselves a test as well as a learning device. Consequently, the syllabus would include within itself a formal assessment of language abilities, which contains an important quality of realism. And this may be a point worth mentioning specifically in publicity for the course. The incidents in a simulation are easily monitored by the teacher, as distinct from monitoring students, for example, going into the streets to interview passers-by. Thus, simulations for assessment purposes provide relatively controlled conditions, a point which is explored later in Chapter 7.

With experience, a little bravery and the right circumstances, the course can be built around simulations, rather than simulations being inserted into the course.

Time

Just as simulations should have a place in the syllabus which reflects their educational value in the course, so also should an individual simulation be allocated adequate time for the introduction, the action and the follow-up.

These days, most language teachers are aware that the simulation technique is valuable. But if the teacher has no experience of using simulations, then there is a temptation to give them the 'Friday afternoon spot', if only as an insurance against things going wrong; in which case the teacher can say that the simulation was introduced as a bit of fun. But students have sensitive antennae for detecting a teacher's educational priorities and values. What occurs may be a self-fulfilling prophesy; an event of little or no educational importance, and perhaps not even a simulation at all, with the students not accepting their roles and playing it for fun. This will then confirm opinions that simulations are not worth much time or trouble. Attitudes have shaped events and events have reinforced attitudes.

It may be, of course, that the simulation is a particularly good one, with in-built safeguards against mistreatment, in which case the experiences may lead the teacher and students to modify their attitudes. But it is unlikely that the simulation experience will be as effective as it would have been if the attitudes had been right in the first place.

There is also a danger of teachers trying to squeeze too much simulation into too little time. Corner cutting, rushing, and a truncated debriefing will diminish the value of the simulation. It may also leave behind a negative or unpleasant impression among the participants. It is one thing to cut a few corners when trying out a simulation with colleagues as a test run; it is quite another to mishandle the time element in the classroom. In general, it is better to allow too much time than too little. A good simulation contains so much language experience that it is quite easy for the extra time to be filled in.

Numbers, space, hardware and costs

The number of participants is rarely a serious difficulty because most simulations are flexible. If it is a small-scale simulation, involving only three or four participants, then it is usually possible to divide a class into groups of three or four and run the same simulation as separate but simultaneous events. This arrangement can work even if a good deal of talking is involved, since the participants can become so engrossed in their own group activities that they are not distracted by a level of noise which might otherwise interfere with their concentration. But if experience shows that there is a noise problem, then an effort can be made to distance the groups as far apart as possible in a single classroom, or to use screens, or to use more than one room.

With small-scale simultaneous simulations, the Controller can usually give everyone the same briefing, and it is desirable that they all take part in the same debriefing, since there are often valuable comparisons to be made about how the different groups tackled the same problem.

If it is a simulation with roles for more participants than the number of students in the class, then the decision about whether to go ahead or not is a technical one. It depends on an examination of the mechanics of the simulation to see whether it would become unbalanced if a role or function were excluded, or if one participant could take on two roles. Perhaps the teacher could bring in one or two students from another class to make up the numbers.

In language classes it may be preferable to choose simulations which have fewer roles than there are students rather than the other way round. Very often it may be an advantage to duplicate a key function; by having two people in the chair, by having two people represent the expert witness, or by having two people as the boss. One person can be an official deputy, or they could both have identical status. Circumstances must decide cases, but experience shows that simulations do offer opportunities for two participants being in the same role, and they back each other up in their exercise of power, responsibility and language.

Space is usually another flexible element. With a little experience of running simulations, the Controller can often use ingenuity to overcome problems of space. The best criteria to use are probably realism and accessibility.

Access takes into account movements among groups, and the movements of the Controller. Realism is a question of the plausibility of such an activity being held in a particular location.

In some cases there is no space problem. All the action may take place in one location with no physical movements of participants around the room – as in the case of a committee-type simulation. A foreign affairs simulation, on the other hand, usually entails separate rooms, or, at worst, groups located in the corners of a single room with a prohibition on eavesdropping and espionage.

Some inter-cultural simulations, such as *Bafá Bafá*, are impossible to run unless there is space for the separate briefings of the two cultures, since members of one culture must not overhear the briefing given to the other culture. This entails two adequately sized rooms, and also two Controllers if the briefings are to take place simultaneously.

Hardware is another aspect which can be considered from the points of view of accessibility and plausibility. In language classes it is often valuable to record the proceedings – on tape or videotape – and this entails the usual technical problems associated with such recordings. Occasionally a simulation incorporates its own plausible need for recording, such as a television simulation, or a public inquiry simulation, where the recording apparatus can be regarded as being inside the simulation event, not outside it. So if it is desirable to record the proceedings, and if there is a choice between two simulations of equal merit, but in one of which a recording would be natural, then that aspect could determine the choice.

All essential hardware is usually listed in the Controller's notes. Non-essential hardware is mentioned in the next chapter, as being part of the preparations for a simulation rather than part of the reasons for the choice of particular simulations.

The cost of simulations varies considerably. Some are free. Some are subsidised by a commercial organisation or an educational institution. Some are produced for a fairly wide market and have a long print run and a relatively low unit cost, whereas other simulations are printed in units, or dozens, as orders come in, and have relatively high costs.

Assuming that there is a reasonable budget for simulations, the question is value for money. What should be avoided is buying a simulation because it is cheap. While a cheap (or free) simulation can be a good one, it can also be a poor one which can put students off the whole idea. With simulations, as with books and educational equipment generally, it may be a good idea to go for quality – to buy one good simulation rather than two indifferent ones. This can be an important consideration in respect of teachers or students who are unfamiliar with simulations. The extra money for a good simulation could be well spent if it not only resulted in a high-quality educational event, but also was the sort of simulation that had been proved to work in a variety of different conditions.

Where to look

As suggested earlier, the wider the choice the more effective the result is likely to be. One of the merits of dipping into non-linguistic areas is that there is likely to be a serendipity value – all sorts of useful ideas can be found by accident.

But in order not to waste a lot of time searching around, it may be a useful first step to find out which particular areas are likely to be the most fruitful. This can be done through a search in the library of an educational institution for books on simulations, especially handbooks which list or describe simulations. Some of these categorise simulations according to their subject matter. A glance at the titles and headings will show the areas which are fertile for simulation design. Economics, business, ecology, geography, social studies, war and politics are all areas where simulations have developed to meet the educational needs.

The simulation technique is a fairly rapidly developing field, with new simulations appearing on the market, while others drop out from the scene. For this reason it can be useful to join a society of simulation users (usually games are included as well as simulations) and the literature of the society will keep the reader up to date. Details of the main societies are given in the bibliography, together with titles of some useful reference books. Another source of up-to-date information is in those practical teacher-orientated language magazines which contain useful hints to the language teacher on materials, methods and techniques.

Unfortunately, much of the literature on simulations, including the writings of authors of simulations, contains some misleading terminology, and various labels seem to be used interchangeably: simulations, games, exercises, role play and so on. So if an activity is labelled a 'game' or an 'exercise', that does not mean it is not a genuine simulation. The label 'simulation' can also be misapplied. When searching for simulations the teacher could well adopt a cautious attitude when examples of mislabelling occur. There is a possibility that the confusion of concept may render the instructions, mechanics, role cards and structured environment less effective than they could be – a point dealt with in detail in Chapter 6, 'Will the simulation work?'

A useful guide in the search for simulations is to take note of authors' names, in the same way as in looking for suitable novels. Authors of simulations have their own styles, and the name of an author can give more information about the quality of a simulation than a description of its aims and contents, or the claims made by the publisher.

Recommended short list

The following list of simulations is short, tentative and personal. It is not intended to be a list of 'best buys', nor is it representative of the many different types of simulation which are available. It is restricted to published simulations which have been well tested. Although some of the simulations in the list contain some faults in design, these are generally minor and should not deter a teacher from considering their use. Some simulations have been included because they are untypical and mind-jogging, as in the case of *Talking Rocks*. Some are relatively short and simple – the author's *Radio Covingham* – while others can last for weeks or months, as in the case of *North Sea Challenge*.

The object of the list is not to restrict choices, but to widen them. By showing a variety of types of simulation it is hoped that the reader will be encouraged to broaden the areas of choice and increase the options for using simulations for language purposes.

BAFÁ BAFÁ

A simulation by Garry Shirts, author of *Starpower*, who is undoubtedly one of the most ingenious and provocative of simulation authors. There are two cassette recordings in this cross-cultural simulation – one for the Alpha culture (warm, friendly, patriarchal) and the other for the Beta culture (foreign-speaking and task orientated). There are artifacts, trading cards, visitors' badges and so on. A simulation eminently suited to teacher training, and advanced level language students. If the briefing is done carefully, then it could be used at intermediate level.

CRISIS

A simulation of international conflict developed in the United States by Western Behavioral Sciences Institute. The participants form teams representing six countries. There are bilateral negotiations, and world conferences. Some role cards stray away from plausibility by being semi-humorous, but the basic situation develops quickly with plenty of interaction. Suitable for advanced students, and also possibly at intermediate level.

FIVE SIMPLE BUSINESS GAMES

These five simulations ('games' is misleading) by Charles Townsend can be used singly or as a series. Their titles are *Gorgeous Gateaux Ltd, Fresh Oven Pies Ltd, Dart Aviation Ltd, The Island Game* and *The Republic Game*. In each of these five simulations the class is divided into four competing groups, representing companies in the first three, and countries in the last two. The first simulation, *Gorgeous Gateaux Ltd,* could even be adapted for use at beginner level, since in each of the five rounds each company takes only two decisions – how much to produce and what price should be charged. The Controller then compares prices, and awards 40 per cent of the market to the company with the lowest price, 30 per cent to the company with the next lowest price, and so on; from these figures each company can work out their profits. There are design faults. It would be better if the four companies had different names; but the teacher can invent them – *Creamy Cakes, Beautiful Buns, Delicious Doughnuts* – rather than each company being called *Gorgeous Gateaux Ltd.*

Also note that the Decision Form says 'Number of orders' when it should say 'Number of crates of cakes produced'. The next four simulations become increasingly complicated, and the last two could hardly be used below advanced level.

HUMANUS

This is not only a provocative survival-type simulation, but an excellent example of how diverse the original intention and the eventual use can be. It was designed by Paul A. Twelker and Kent Layden specifically for the study of futurology, yet probably not one teacher in a thousand uses it for this reason. It concerns ethical and social values; the participants being survivors of a world-wide catastrophe, and their link with the outside world being a 'voice print-out of a computer' (cassette recording). It lasts between one and two hours, and virtually any number can participate. Suitable for advanced level and teacher training.

MAN AND HIS ENVIRONMENT

A popular simulation at intermediate and advanced level about a number of potential industrial and commercial developments. The area involved is illustrated on a board. There are role cards, of only a few sentences each, for opponents and proponents of each development. Although in some cases the background information is too skimpy to enable satisfactory decisions to be made, it can produce plenty of interaction.

NORTH SEA CHALLENGE

This three-part simulation by Michael Lynch has design faults, but plenty of technical data and excellent artwork. It is described in detail in Chapter 6, 'Will the simulation work?' Produced by British Petroleum Educational Service, it has an interesting history. It was intended for native sixth form students (17 plus) interested in technological decision making. But EFL teachers discovered it and found it useful at advanced level. They persuaded BP to produce an accompanying language pack. However, this pack cost considerably more than the simulation itself and was later abandoned by BP when it was found that it did not sell well, and that those teachers who bought it seldom bought the simulation itself.

RADIO COVINGHAM

A media simulation by the author, suitable for advanced and intermediate level. It is a fully participatory simulation, and one of the author's *Nine Graded Simulations*, designed to encourage language and communication skills and originally published by the Inner London Education Authority. There are 'Notes for Participants', which explain that the participants are journalists on the local radio station, Radio Covingham, who have to produce a ten-minute programme, called 'News and Views at Seven', from handouts, listeners' letters, and news items which flow in during the course of the simulation. There is a map of the area and a Station Manager's memo complaining of what happened a few days ago and giving advice on how to interview people effectively.

TALKING ROCKS

This was written by Robert F. Vernon, an expert on prehistoric petroglyphs and pictographs, with the help and advice of Garry Shirts. It is a good example of simulations which are both simple and sophisticated, suitable for children and professors. It is described in detail in Chapter 6. It is suitable for intermediate level and upwards.

These eight simulations work well in a variety of learning situations, and are not too simple in decision-making aspects. Like most good simulations they can be used with wide ranges of age and mental ability. For language students certain aspects may need modification in certain circumstances. Any combination of these simulations would be suitable examples in teacher training. Details of publication are given in the bibliography.

Checklist of criteria for choosing simulations

1 Decide on the priority of aims – icebreakers, assessment and so on.
2 Estimate the interactive language competence of the students.
3 Search for simulations in as wide an area as possible.
4 If the language level of a simulation is suitable, then examine the mechanics of the simulation – time, numbers, interactive possibilities and so on.
5 If it seems to be a suitable choice, then participate in it yourself first.
6 Consider whether it needs adapting, bearing in mind the dangers of over-adaptation, which are discussed in the next chapter.

3 Preparing for the simulation

Teacher participation

At some stage between looking around for a suitable simulation and introducing it to the students, the teacher should participate in it. The reason is to avoid disasters, and to improve the presentation of the simulation. Since a simulation is an event, and a structured event which requires some preparation by the teacher, it is important that preparation should be based on inside experience, and not on a hopeful guess about what might happen based on reading the materials.

Teacher participation can be regarded as a two-phase assessment. Firstly, the teacher does not simply read the documents, but takes an imaginary journey into what it would be like to have one of the functions. This involves imagining how much reading needs to be done in that role, how much has already been explained by the Controller, what the problem is, what the options for taking action are, and which other participants would help in the task. If there are two or three key roles, then the teacher can take each role in turn. In this way the teacher can form an idea of the reading required (for learning or for reference); the type of writing (note-taking or formal preparation); the type of listening and speaking (informal chats or formal speech); and the type of action (simple decision making or sophisticated interaction).

This first phase should be sufficient to reduce the number of possible simulations to a convenient short list. The second phase is physical interactive participation with colleagues or friends, or, as suggested in the last chapter, perhaps with a formal or informal guinea pig club. By trying it out in practice, even if a few corners are cut, the teacher will be in a much better position to handle the simulation in the classroom. The interactive participation can reveal possible sticking points, unclear details, inadequate instructions and problems involving passive or part-time roles. It can also reveal imaginative options, exciting interaction, and opportunities for the development of language and communication skills. It should also be a useful test run of the mechanics: who sits where, which documents should be handed out when, and how long should be allowed for each period. Teacher participation can either be in the function of Controller or as one of the student participants. If it is a simulation with two or three stages, then roles might be switched after each stage.

In almost all cases, the trial run should follow closely the instructions and advice of the author. Any modifications or adaptations should come later – based on experience, not guesswork.

Adapting

The first thing that should be said about adapting is that it can be dangerous. Leaving out bits which do not appear to be essential can cause all sorts of problems if their function had been to stop things going wrong. Hasty and in-experienced adaptation can ruin a good simulation. Another danger is that if the adaptation involves photocopying and reproducing the documents or adapted documents of an author's work, it can be illegal – a breach of copyright.

Adaptation for geographical reasons is almost always a mistake. If the simulation has authentic-type materials, then to change all the geographical names to those of the locality where the simulation occurs is to sacrifice this authenticity by using documents of inferior quality. Also, geographical changes can destroy the balance of the simulation by importing local conventions and customs, which pre-empt arguments or turn the simulation into a debate on local affairs. Changing the locality of the simulation destroys the convention that the only 'facts' are in the documents. This could lead to a great deal of argument about whether a particular local condition is a fact or not; an argument which is outside the simulation and involves a suspension of the reality of function while the 'rules' are debated. Changing the continent, country, or city of the location of a simulation suggests that the teacher has misconceived the purpose of the simulation. It is not intended to teach local facts; this can be better achieved by other means. Books, novels, plays and poems are not adapted by classroom teachers for the same reason; there is no point in changing *The Merchant of Venice* into *The Merchant of London* or *The Merchant of Rio*. It would be time-consuming and the result would be inferior to the original.

This leaves two major areas for suitable adaptation – for language and for mechanics. How this should be done depends on experience, particularly the experience of the trial run. In general it is better to under-modify than over-modify.

Adapting the mechanics of a simulation is aimed at making it function more effectively in the conditions in which it is used. For example, the simulation may stipulate that one person should be given the role of chairman, or scientific expert, or managing director. Depending on the ability of the participants, it might be a good idea to have two people share a particular key role. They could help each other with problems of vocabulary, grammar, pronunciation, and could back each other up on procedural points.

If the language in the briefing documents (or cassette recording) is too advanced for the students, then there are several ways of modifying this. In *Bafá Bafá*, where the briefing is by cassette, the teacher could also use the printed text side by side with the voice, stopping the tape for additional explanations whenever desirable. If the simulation documents themselves are too complicated, then probably the wrong simulation has been chosen. So the difficulty will usually lie in one document, or a section of a document. Rather than rewrite the document, which would lose authenticity, it would probably be better for the teacher to produce an additional document – of general plausibility – to explain the difficult part. Alternatively, the teacher can explain the difficulty before the action begins. More examples of the actual mechanics of specific simulations, and how they might be adapted, are contained in Chapter 6, 'Will the simulation work?'

The best rule is that if in doubt, do not adapt. Teachers tend to overestimate the difficulties in simulations, and underestimate the motivation and self-help which occur. Also, the aim is not perfection, it is practice. Other things being equal, it is useful to start from the assumption that the simulation has been tried and tested many times, and that the author has got it right. For the first time at least, use it in accordance with the instructions. If the result shows it needs adaptation, then the adaptation can be confidently based on experience.

An overview briefing

Once a simulation has been chosen, tested and perhaps adapted, the next step will depend on whether or not the students are familiar with simulations. If they are not familiar with the technique, then it is worth while spending half an hour or so on general explanation and discussion, interspersed with examples of specific simulations which illustrate the wide variety of subject matter, and the different types of language, communication and organisational skills involved. The teacher can select ideas and examples from this book, and the Key Reminders should be a useful checklist.

Experience has shown that the usual problem is not that the students are ignorant of what a simulation is, but that they think it is something different. The problem is not learning; it is unlearning and relearning, and that is more difficult.

Fortunately, the simulation concept is simple and consistent. It is centred on the ideas of reality of function; of power and ownership; of duties and responsibilities. It is not concerned with theatre, or with games, or with the way engineers use the word simulation – to mean a mock-up, working model, or even mathematical formulae. It is worth pointing out the traps of terminology: of using words and phrases such as 'acting', 'playing', 'staging', 'having fun', 'fun and games', 'acting it out' and so forth. The danger is that the wrong words create false expectations, and false expectations cause inappropriate behaviour.

In giving an overview of simulations, the teacher might stress the absolute necessity of role acceptance. Without role acceptance there is no simulation.

If the participants start acting parts, or fooling around, then they have abandoned their roles and their duties and responsibility. They have, in effect, sacked themselves, and the simulation lies dead on the classroom floor. Even though the activity may continue, it is no longer a simulation that is occurring. Stress that 'facts' cannot be invented to win arguments. The relevant facts are in the documents. The participants are not inventors or authors; they are not actors or magicians. They have to fulfil their functions the best they can with the facts at their disposal.

A problem which may occur with students who are new to simulations is that they just cannot believe that they have the power which has been given to them. Even if they are used to taking part in role play, exercises, games and so forth in language learning, it can still come as something of a surprise to realise just how wide their powers can be within the structure of a simulation. Some participants in their first simulation may feel uncomfortable, unsure that their functions include the powers that are normally conferred by such functions in the world outside the classroom. 'Are we allowed to...?' is a question which may crop up. These questions are often procedural. 'Can the chairman suspend the sitting?' 'Can the other committee members move a vote of no confidence in the chairman?'

The teacher can make the general point that if the participants are ever in any doubt about the extent of their powers, they should ask themselves whether such powers are normally inherent in the function. If they are, then those are the powers they have in the simulation. However, the teacher can also explain that the powers are dependent upon the acceptance of the function, duties and responsibilities of the role. A participant in the role of statesman, for example, has not the power to become a magician and invent facts to suit his purposes. And a corollary of participant power is that they are on their own inside the simulation, and cannot ask the Controller for help in decision making.

Thus, the overview briefing should cover all of the three essential aspects of a simulation contained in the definition 'A simulation is reality of function in a simulated and structured environment.'

On the question of language and social and communicative skills, the teacher can suit the overview briefing to the needs of the circumstances. A general point well worth emphasising is the importance of the simulation technique as a practice ground for language skills. Nor is it simply a matter of skills. Confidence and human relations are involved and are often just as important as the skills themselves.

Specific briefing

Although the overview briefing probably dispelled any notion that a simulation is another name for a game, role play, or informal drama, it is still worth while for the inexperienced Controller to concentrate on using suitable labels, and to avoid using words with misleading associations. While it is difficult to draw a precise line between the acceptable and the misleading, the following list might be useful:

Suitable	*Unsuitable*
Simulation	Drama, role play, game, exercise
Controller	Teacher
Participants	Students, players, actors
Situation, environment	Scene, drama
Mechanics	Rules, stage directions, move, turn, go
Identity, function	Part, character, role
Behaviour, function	Perform, pretend, act, mimic, stage, play, play-act, enact, invent, create
Duty, responsibility, outcome	Win, lose, score, points
Role card, profile	Role-play card, personality card

So pervasive is the vocabulary of gaming and the theatre that the use of some of the unsuitable words will be very difficult to avoid. And even in this book, the word 'role' is sometimes used as synonymous with 'identity' or 'function', and it is commonly used in simulation literature. But the odd mislabelling will not matter provided the Controller clearly distinguishes the concept of the simulation technique.

The need to get the words right is not semantic dogmatism; it is in order to avoid a mishmash activity, in which some participants are functioning seriously, while the others are having fun, playing games, pretending, acting out their roles, inventing facts, or else are inhibited because they think it is a guided exercise and are overly conscious of the 'teacher'. Such activity would not be a simulation, and a good deal of ill feeling may result from the conflict of motives and behaviour. A little practice – including that of the trial run – should be enough to deal with the problem of terminology. This leaves only the major task of the briefing, which is explaining the mechanics.

In briefing a specific simulation, the Controller should provide enough information for the participants to understand what is involved, but not so much that it starts to pre-empt their decision making. The Controller should point out that the participants have full powers to do anything that would seem sensible or plausible in the situation, but the Controller should refrain from making suggestions, and even giving options, regarding specific decision making.

If, in order to explain a general point, the Controller wishes to give specific examples, then the examples should be fictitious ones, which are not related directly to the 'facts' in the simulation. This advice may be difficult to follow, since the teacher may wish to improve the result of the simulation by suggesting specific lines of thought and conduct which would aid the participants. But with each additional hint and piece of advice, the simulation is becoming less of a simulation, and the power of the participants is being gradually eroded. While appearing to help, the teacher is actually removing the essence of ownership, and changing the category to that of a rehearsed event.

The Controller should stay well clear of the decision-making field, and concentrate on the mechanics. For example, supposing a simulation involves a board of management meeting, and the Controller's notes say only 'The board of management should meet and discuss what to do about this problem.' The mechanics, which should be explained in the briefing, concern the timing (when the meeting should start and finish); the procedures (whether there should be a chairman, an agenda, a voting procedure); the location of the meeting ('three tables joined together at that end of the room'); plus any suggestions for name tags, carafe of water, note pads and pencils, charts, documents and so forth.

In dealing with these points in the briefing, the Controller is trying to ensure that the action runs smoothly. Otherwise, the simulation may become derailed. Perhaps like this:

'Mr Chairman, I don't think you should have the power to decide this issue by yourself.'
'I think we should have a vote.'
'What do we normally do?'
'I don't know. Let's ask the Controller.'

And later.

'Yes, that's all right, the Controller says we can take a vote.'
'Is it by simple majority, or does it have to be two thirds or something?'
'It must be by simple majority.'
'Yes, but the chairman has the casting vote.'
'What?'
'If there is a tie, then I vote again, and that decides it.'
'That's not fair.'
'Let's ask the Controller.'

These procedural issues could be anticipated and clarified in advance. Moreover, if this is done in one or two simulations, the precedents could remain in force in subsequent simulations where the same type of meeting occurs.

Another general point which can be made in the briefing is the need to respect the facts, and not to invent facts to win arguments. It is often useful for the Controller to give a few imaginary examples of what is not allowed:

'Now, the residents object to the proposal to build the nuclear power station. They may feel upset about this proposal, but they have to rely on the facts as given in the documents. They cannot invent an official report which says the ground is contaminated by anthrax, or is on an earthquake fault, or is located on an old arms dump. They are residents, not inventors.'

'The leaders of the three governments cannot start a war or even start a demonstration. They can issue orders for a war, or for a demonstration, or a day of prayer; but whether these orders are carried out is decided by the Controller. But they can negotiate treaties, give news conferences, or issue an ultimatum, and the

Controller will arrange the mechanics for these events, but will not interfere with the content of the treaties, news conferences and so on.'

'Espionage is not allowed. There are no spies. Each group is separated by hundreds of miles, and cannot see or hear what the other groups are doing. If you hear one group talking too loudly, then report it to the Controller, since this is a problem in the mechanics of the simulation, and I'll then try to move the other group further away, or ask them to speak more quietly.'

There are usually several general points which should be made about the documents. Can they be written on? Should they be treated with care so that they can be used again? Are they available for the whole of the simulation, or for only part of it? Advice may be needed on confidential documents. Do the participants have discretionary powers to reveal what is contained in their own confidential documents, and even show the documents to others? Or is the confidentiality obligatory; a secret which must not be disclosed to others? What are the mechanics for ensuring confidentiality – simply turning the documents upside down on the desk when other participants come near; or is there some place of safe keeping?

Some simulations involve different stages. The Controller can decide whether to give a single briefing, or mini-briefings between stages. If the simulation involves changing the classroom furniture around, then it is sometimes helpful for the Controller to come to the simulation armed with diagrams showing which group sits where in each stage. Such diagrams reduce the dangers of muddle and confusion with the Controller saying 'No, take that chair there, not there, and leave enough space here.'

If the briefing is not immediately followed by the simulation, then this gives the participants time to think about what they will have to do, and mentally prepare themselves. With some simulations this can be a good idea. It also allows the participants the opportunity to make suggestions which otherwise might be too late to be accepted: 'I can get a large sheet which we could use as a placard', or 'Shall we write out our own name tags for our countries, like they have at the United Nations?'

If the briefing is to be followed immediately by the simulation, then it is vital that the Controller should ensure that all required documents are present. Experience shows that this advice is necessary. An attitude of 'I'm pretty busy, but I think I have everything' is risky. Extra copies of document X will not compensate for an inadequate number of copies of document Y. If one document out of ten is missing, then this does not mean a 10 per cent reduction in simulation effectiveness; it may be like pulling out one can from the bottom of a pile of cans. Not only would it affect the balance of the simulation; it may make it inoperable. A 'Sorry, we can't do it today' may be bad, but to get half-way through the simulation and realise that a vital document is missing would be even worse.

Role allocation

In thinking about role allocation, it is important for the language teacher to remember that the Controller is not a casting director, that a simulation is not a play, and that opportunities for language learning may be circumscribed by the Controller trying to manipulate the roles in order to achieve the 'best performance'. If the teacher thinks that only student A can take role X, and only student B is capable of handling role Y, then the simulation has been badly chosen, and it would be preferable to look elsewhere.

To manipulate role allocation in order to achieve what may or may not turn out to be marginal improvements is extremely unwise. It contradicts the essential nature of a simulation, which is not to achieve the best possible result, but to give everyone an opportunity of fair and full participation. It embroils the Controller in a personal selection process which may be resented by those who are chosen for a specific role as well as by those who are not chosen. Manipulation also encroaches on participant ownership of a simulation; it reduces status and self-respect; and instead of reality of function there may be resentment of function, perhaps leading to disaffection or even sabotage.

It is true, of course, that a random role allocation will probably result in key roles being filled by some of the less able students; not only in their ability to use language, but also in their organisational abilities – since chance alone will be the determining factor. The teacher's attitude should not be 'What a pity, but perhaps I can manipulate the role allocation by deceit', but rather 'Thank goodness for mistakes, errors and misunderstandings, for without these the learning experience would be far less valuable.' An additional point is that in life it is not always the most able who are in charge. In life, key roles are not always allocated to those best able to fulfil the functions. If there really is a role which is very demanding and isolated (perhaps the role of an expert who has to produce facts and figures), then the most appropriate method would be to arrange for two participants to occupy this role, both chosen at random.

Another problem – the reverse of the first – is whether the role allocation should be manipulated to keep the most appropriate person out of a specific role. If a language student really is a managing director, then the Controller may feel it would be preferable that he should not be given this role in a simulation. While this is a less serious problem than the first one, it is still better to allocate by chance, unless the person concerned is opposed to taking his chance with the others.

Where manipulation of roles is acceptable is when a simulation is rerun. In this case, the landlords can become the tenants, the workers can become the management, and so forth; but all are still being treated equally, and the Controller is in no danger of making invidious personal selections.

There are various methods of random selection, but whichever method is chosen it should be seen to be random, and advertised as being random. One method is to place the role cards face down on the table and allow the participants to pick up their own cards. Another technique is to draw numbers or name tags out of a hat. A common method is for the Controller to 'count off' the students one by one as they are seated in the classroom. If the Controller has to establish a specific number of groups, say five, then in counting off the students each student is given a number from 1 to 5. Groups are then formed by students of the same given number gathering together. If, on the other hand, there have to be several groups with a specific number of participants in each group, say three, then students are simply counted off in threes, each three being a group.

Random methods are not only fair, and are seen to be fair, but they also avoid time wasting and squabbling, which often occur if the students are asked to volunteer for roles. The volunteer method is unsatisfactory because it gives an unfair advantage to the extroverts by allowing them to get in first and pick the 'best' roles, or probably the 'easiest' roles, leaving the other students to take what remains. Even if the extroverts were mistaken in their choices, it still leaves the shy, polite and less articulate students feeling that they enter the simulation with inferior status.

As mentioned earlier, if one or two students object to random allocation because it breaks up their friendship groups, then the teacher can explain that language skills need to be practised between everyone, not just between friends. And from the teacher's point of view, random allocation has the virtue of breaking up cliques and increasing personal contacts between students.

Language briefing

Experienced language teachers who have no experience of simulations are likely to be tempted not only to give a language briefing before a simulation, but to overdo it.

A language briefing has several potential disadvantages. It may make some students too inhibited to say anything rather than deviate from the forms and patterns of speech practised in the language briefing. It may induce anxieties which diminish participant responsibility by emphasising teacher expectations, so that instead of trying to function within a situation as best they can, the participants will be thinking of the 'teacher' being present. If they think of themselves as being students, then it will not be a genuine simulation.

For language purposes, the aim of a simulation is not to produce the correct words, grammar and pronunciation, but to communicate effectively according to roles, functions and duties. And because a language briefing would immediately precede a simulation, there is a very real danger that instead of the students relying on their general knowledge of the language, they will be plagued by the intrusive thought 'How did the teacher, just now, tell us we were supposed to say this?'

If the language briefing is used by the teacher in an attempt to prescribe the language input, then this is a straightforward category mistake. There can be no dictating of language input in a simulation, since it would reduce or remove the power of the participants to say whatever they thought was most effective in the circumstances. If the chosen simulation is not beyond the general competence of the students, then it is advisable to leave language questions to the debriefing.

In most cases, the key issue is the mechanics: will the simulation work if there is no language briefing? If the question is one of vocabulary, then the points to be considered are whether the simulation involves groups, when one participant can help another; whether the documents containing the unusual words have them in contexts which allow intelligent guesses; and whether these unusual words are key concepts. With most language briefings it should not be necessary to give more than half a dozen word meanings. The students should then be encouraged to try to work out any other meanings for themselves during the action, and only to ask the Controller if there is serious doubt about an important word.

Another type of language briefing is justified when the simulation involves a particular formal activity, and the students are anxious to use the correct forms of address. If it is to be a simulation about a court case, then how should a judge be addressed – 'Your lordship', 'Your honour', 'M'lud', 'Most learned judge', or 'Sir'? If the country is specified in the simulation and the Controller knows the answer, then the correct form of address can be used. If the country is not specified, or is fictitious, or the teacher does not know the answer if it is an actual country, then the language briefing can be used to discuss the most appropriate form of address in the circumstances, and this form can be used in the simulation. If it is a parliamentary simulation, then the language briefing can discuss appropriate forms of parliamentary language – 'Mr Speaker', 'Honourable Members', 'Distinguished Senators' and so forth. Not only does such discussion assist in the realism and formality of the occasion, but it also enables the Controller to use flattering titles to address the participants – 'Would the noble and distinguished members of the Goodland Parliament please assemble to hear the message from the most honourable Head of State?' This is much better than saying 'Would you students come and sit here?' There should be no need for any preliminary language briefing for informal modes of speech; such points can be dealt with in the debriefing.

A language briefing, like the question of adaptation, works well when based on experience of simulations in the language classroom. For the inexperienced Controller, it is better to take a relaxed attitude and do too little rather than do too much.

4 The simulation in action

The Controller

Although a simulation is not taught, the teacher, as Controller, is the most important person during a simulation.

But the control is similar to that of a traffic controller: a person who controls the flow of traffic, tries to avoid bottlenecks, but does not tell individual motorists the direction of their journeys. Decision making, problem solving and interaction are the responsibility of the participants, but it is the Controller who has the job of making it all possible.

For the Controller, the action can be a most pleasant and relaxing experience. All the difficult work has been done: the choosing, the preparation and the briefing. Apart from the first simulation, when the participants may feel uncertain about what they can and cannot do, simulations tend to run themselves. Providing the briefing has been adequate, the Controller can sit back and enjoy the experience. The problem is not to keep the simulation going, but to stop it early enough to allow adequate time for the debriefing. If there is no possibility of an extension of time, then the Controller should keep to the pre-arranged timetable for each stage.

As the students become more familiar with simulations, they will not only become more adept at their functions within the action, but will also help organise the mechanics. Ownership of the decision making will increase their self-respect and sense of responsibility, and this will spill over into Control areas. Teachers who use simulations regularly sometimes abdicate their role of Controller, and let one or two of the students organise the mechanics of the simulations – letting them take it in turns in order to give them experience. This leaves the teacher completely free to monitor the language, behaviour and social skills in the action.

Teachers who are controlling their first simulation are often surprised by the absence of teaching duties. Instead of the eye-to-eye, mind-to-mind, teacher–student stimulus and response, with all its tensions and attentions, the initial reaction is one of strangeness, as though a large burden had been shed. Suddenly there is no teacher and no students. Old habits may be hard to overcome, and the Controller may think 'Shouldn't I be teaching them something? Do they know what they are doing?' Observation may also bring some surprises. Some students who are too shy to make voluntary utterances in class might be observed arguing a policy. Students who are usually polite to the point of 'correctness' may be observed behaving with more informality, or else engaged in a heated discussion.

The greatest danger for the Controller is to interfere in the action unnecessarily. It is one thing to interfere in order to make some change in the mechanics of the simulation – perhaps to adjust the seating arrangements or extend a time limit – but it is quite another thing to sit down in a group and say 'How are you getting on?' Unnecessary interference damages simulations. Often, the temptation is difficult to resist, but it should be resisted. The Controller should avoid smiles, frowns, hints and gestures which indicate encouragement or discouragement of decision-making behaviour. Each bit of interference diminishes participant responsibility and reinserts the teacher into the classroom. Instead of looking at each other, the participants will start looking at the Controller, or even looking over their shoulders at the Controller. With more interference, the Controller becomes the teacher, the participants become the students, and the result is a teacher-assassinated simulation.

The Controller may feel that interference for language reasons is justifiable, since the main aim is to assist language learning. Again, this is a serious category mistake, and is likely to be counter-productive. Instead of helping language, it will tend to interrupt the thoughts of the participants, jerk them out of their functions and duties, diminish their sense of status and ownership, and inhibit their use of language. Unless a participant makes a language error that is so serious it hinders the smooth running of the simulation, then the Controller should simply make a note of the language point and raise it in the debriefing.

Controlling the behaviour of the participants is not the Controller's job. They control themselves. But misbehaviour, or inappropriate behaviour, is another matter, since it affects the mechanics of the simulation.

If one or two participants start fooling around or playing it for laughs or sit sunk in depression or apathy, then they have abandoned their duties and responsibilities. They are no longer in their roles. They have sacked themselves and are not part of the simulation. In these circumstances, the Controller should act as guardian of the simulation, but within the simulation conventions. The most effective way is to send a note to the participant from the editor, managing director, head of state, or whoever might be appropriate, asking them to withdraw for an urgent meeting. This gives the Controller a chance to find out what the matter is. The explanation might have nothing to do with the simulation. It might be toothache, or personal ill feeling between students. The cause of the trouble may be misunderstanding about the nature of the role, or the participant may have nothing to do and has become dissatisfied. There are various remedies according to circumstances. The participant could re-enter the simulation with the misunderstanding cleared up, or return in another role, or to another group, or else help the Controller with the mechanics of the simulation, and so on.

If the worst comes to the worst, and most or all of the participants start playing around, or inventing facts to win arguments, or indulging in amateur dramatics, then the simulation is long since dead and awaits burial. Certainly the Controller should never stand idly by and allow a shouting match to develop. The activity should be stopped forthwith. The question is how it came about in the first place. Was it a bad simulation? Was it badly briefed? Were there external elements which had nothing to do with the simulation? Moreover, such an extraordinary occurrence does not arise in a moment; it has to develop. Foul play is met by retaliation, and this leads to further disruption. In other words, a chain of unusual events is taking place, all of which are non-simulation events. They are contrary to role acceptance. So, unless the Controller is asleep, there is no danger of massive misbehaviour; it is dealt with well before it reaches that stage.

One of the reasons why bad behaviour does not occur in any but the most exceptional circumstances is that the participants do not want it to occur. They have an investment in the simulation, and they do not want it sabotaged. Also, they do not need to wait for Controller intervention – they have the powers and functions necessary for dealing with potential sabotage themselves. It is not unusual in simulations to find subtle pressures at work which ensure role acceptance. A sudden change of tone, a formal mode of address, a sharp glance, can all serve as warning signals by participants to an individual who is moving towards unacceptable forms of behaviour. If these warnings are ignored, the participants have more overt and powerful methods of control: verbal warnings, appeals to the authorities within the simulation, points of order, and threats of sanctions. And in the last resort they can appeal directly to the Controller.

What the Controller should look for is the position of heads. Are the heads together in avid discussion? Is one head withdrawn, isolated, and looking out of the window? Is one group sitting doing nothing, all looking one way, and becoming impatient or bored? Lack of involvement indicates that the mechanics may be going wrong. One group may have finished well before the others. If so, then the Controller should do something about it; preferably having anticipated the event in advance and having prepared a way of getting the group back into the simulation. Circumstances must decide cases. If, for example, one participant is sitting isolated and waiting to be interviewed, then although seemingly not involved with the action, the candidate may be mentally very involved indeed, rehearsing the answers to anticipated questions.

The Controller could also make a self-assessment. 'Am I standing rigidly, nervously playing with a pencil? Am I distracting the participants by pacing rapidly up and down, thrusting documents here and there? Or am I relaxed, inconspicuous and confident?'

Monitoring the functional behaviour

In this book 'function' refers to appropriate behaviour, and this depends on the nature of the job and the circumstances. It thus includes a wide variety of behaviour – organisational, communicative, social, and even antisocial on occasions – depending on the particular situation.

So, in order for the Controller to monitor the function effectively, it is important to know the basic circumstances which exist at the moment the simulation starts. In other words, the Controller should have a good knowledge of the documents being used in the simulation, plus a practical knowledge gained from a trial run of what it is like to be in the hot seat. This threshold knowledge means that the Controller starts off by knowing what each participant is trying to achieve, and what resources are available for this task. In general terms the functioning is predictable, but in particular terms the behaviour of individual participants faced with a task can differ widely. However, because the Controller starts the monitoring with the shared knowledge of the situation, and since the behaviour as well as the language will be cohesive, the job of monitoring the function is not difficult.

The monitoring includes not only what is done, but also what is not done. In the transcript given later of *Space Crash* it will be noticed that some participants failed to throw into the general pool of information all the facts on their role cards. If the Controller is giving exclusive attention to one group only, then this is the sort of thing that can be noticed. Even if the monitoring is intermittent, with the Controller moving from group to group, the participants themselves will often indicate functional failings. 'Has anyone got any information about...?' is the sort of question that occurred in *Space Crash*, and it occurs in other simulations which include individual role cards.

When participants begin their first simulation, they may not bother about organisation. They may start their discussion of the details of a problem immediately; not thinking that it might be a good idea to organise themselves first, draw up an agenda, divide up the tasks, define their objectives, and list their resources. However, at some stage or other in the first simulation, and certainly by the time the second and third simulations come along, the participants will have learned from experience. And this learning adds to the cohesive nature of the behaviour, and makes it easier for the Controller to monitor what is going on.

The monitoring of behaviour is no esoteric skill. Everyone does it. It is often both automatic and unconscious. We are often unaware of our subtle monitoring of behavioural signals, including body language, monitoring not only what is done but also what is omitted. But we are aware of our general impressions, which are based on these subtle monitorings. With practice of monitoring simulations a Controller can become more aware of particular subtleties of behaviour, and this can be valuable on occasions, but it is an additional skill, not an essential skill. The main objective is to form general impressions based on knowledge of the starting point, plus the actual paths taken by the participants to reach their objectives.

Often the Controller has a choice between closely observing one group of participants, or making a general but less detailed observation of all the groups. This is a matter for the personal judgement of the Controller. A useful technique for monitoring more than one group at a time is to move around the classroom very slowly, avoiding eye contact, but listening. After a short time the participants disregard the monotonous movements of their Controller. Experience of using several simulations with the same group of students makes it easier for the Controller to decide whether to try to monitor one group, or several. With the first simulation the Controller is not sure what to expect, but with experience of several simulations the Controller finds that behaviour starts falling into patterns, and is easier to monitor effectively.

There is one type of simulation which needs very careful monitoring, and that is the type which deliberately involves personalities in order to demonstrate something about human relationships. This type can include the cross-cultural simulations which have the theme of emotional conflict (see Chapter 2), or they can be psychological simulations in which the participants are encouraged or provoked into revealing attitudes and emotions that are not part of their normal everyday behaviour.

Garry Shirts' *Starpower* is the classic example of a provocative simulation of this type, which starts as though it were a trading game, but half-way through the 'successful' group is told that it can change the rules if it wishes to do so. Depending on the wealth and status of their groups, participants can feel surges of rage, greed, envy, revolt, or smug superiority. This sometimes results in highly emotional scenes. Other simulations, using more direct (and cruder) methods, can produce real hatred among participants, which can even escalate into violence.

Such simulations should not be chosen in the first place unless the Controller is confident of handling any emotional outbursts. So the main problem is to monitor carefully the signs of tension and hostility, and then jump in and stop the simulation before blows are struck, or hatred takes too great a hold. In such simulations, the debriefing (or defusing) is particularly important in order to draw lessons from the experience. Consequently, the Controller should pay particular attention to the behaviour as it develops during the action so that the observations can be used effectively in the debriefing. Providing the Controller pays attention to what is going on, the actual task of monitoring such behaviour is not difficult for the reasons mentioned when discussing simulations in general: the behaviour is cohesive, and the Controller starts off with a knowledge of the documents, the roles and functions, and the likely way the simulation will develop.

Monitoring the language

Listening tends to be an undervalued skill. Since it has the appearance of being passive, and since the main action occurs in the mind of the listener, it is sometimes assumed to be easy. Listening can be, and often is, a highly skilled occupation. The listening of a judge to a court case is one example of this skill. The listening of the drama critic, the orchestral conductor, and the naval sonar operator are all professional skills.

In monitoring the language used during a simulation, the Controller will be using the professional skills of a language teacher. The type of language which the Controller monitors is a matter for professional judgement, depending on the syllabus, the students and the aims. The Controller can pay specific attention to certain modes of speech; whether the participants get their tenses right; whether they make adequate use of conditionals, modal auxiliaries and so forth. Specific attention can be paid to particular participants. The Controller may wish to compare students' abilities to deal with unexpected behavioural problems. Attention could be concentrated on social language. Or, instead of monitoring for pre-specified objectives, the Controller can simply listen and take mental note of (or jot down) points of interest as they arise.

The type of monitoring may well be determined by the reason for using that particular simulation. If it is icebreaking, then the Controller can concentrate on behavioural language – the language of action and interaction. If the simulation is used for cross-cultural purposes, then attention is likely to be on the way the participants match the language with their cultural objectives. If it is to assess the participants' ability to understand and act upon written or printed documents, then the Controller's notebook could contain a list of the relevant documents, and notes about how they were used. For a more thorough analysis of discourse during the simulation, it is best to make a recording of the proceedings. In Chapter 5, the section entitled 'Analysing simulation discourse' shows how a transcript can be analysed (a) for grammar, and (b) for functional effectiveness.

Probably the most likely general use of monitoring is to use the observations as and when appropriate in subsequent lessons. In this case the Controller need feel none of the tension which might be present if the aim were to produce instant analysis for the debriefing.

Monitoring is also an inevitable function of the participants themselves, and part of the nature of the simulation technique, since events are causal, and one thing follows another because of the interaction and reaction to ideas, suggestions, arguments and so on. Unlike writing an answer in an examination, the participant usually knows immediately if the language is effective or not. A glance at the analysis of discourse in Chapter 5 will show many examples of instantaneous reaction. One participant says: 'I know there is a kind of – the grass – er – the bran, and we have to...' 'The bran?' interjects another participant. Participants are constantly monitoring other people's language, and also their own, out of functional necessity.

Participant monitoring is probably more important than the monitoring by the Controller, since it is more detailed and personal. Also, it becomes stored memory, and can be recollected in tranquillity, when some of the main lessons can be learned. The Controller's monitoring is more professional and more impartial, and should, in the debriefing or later, be used to complement the impressions of language in use which the participants remember from the simulation experiences.

5 The follow-up

Debriefing for behaviour

The language teacher can think about the debriefing in two ways: the sort of debriefing which occurs when participants are using their own native language in a simulation, and the extra elements in a debriefing which occurs when the participants are using a foreign language.

With native speakers a debriefing may be concerned only with behaviour, whereas in a language class the emphasis may be on debriefing for linguistic reasons. However, because of the wide variety of situations and students, of aims and achievements, there can be a great deal of flexibility. Native speakers may be inarticulate mumblers who are unable to communicate effectively in groups, and the teacher may use a simulation solely for language reasons. Similarly, a language teacher may focus attention entirely on behaviour in the debriefing, perhaps to demonstrate the different behaviours of different cultures, different societies and different philosophies.

Even when the aims of teachers may differ, the mechanics of the debriefing may be similar. For example, whether the aim of the debriefing is to investigate language or behaviour, it can be useful to start the debriefing by asking each participant in turn to explain briefly what they did and why. This achieves a double object. It continues the practice of communication and language skills, and it also puts everyone in the picture about what happened. With different groups operating in a simulation, the students will be keen to know what went on in the other groups. Even if the participants were all in one group, and everyone saw and heard everything, it is still interesting to learn something about what went on in the minds of the participants – how they viewed the problem, and why they decided to do what they did. Moreover, the procedure for taking it in turns to give a brief explanation – without discussion – continues the practice of fair play and equal opportunities, power and responsibility, which characterises the simulation technique. It puts the emphasis on the learner.

The next stage of the debriefing can take many forms. The Controller may wish to explain points about the mechanics of the simulation: why the meeting had to be cut short or more time allowed, or the reason for the decision to have the witnesses standing up when giving evidence, rather than sitting down.

If the participants are new to the simulation technique, then the Controller – now back in the role of teacher – is likely to take charge of the debriefing and guide the discussion. But with experienced participants it may be a good idea to place a student (perhaps with an assistant) in the chair. In some circumstances the teacher may give precise instructions to the chairpersons about the procedure for conducting the debriefing and the subject areas to be covered in the discussion, whereas in other cases the students may be able to tackle the job effectively without any guidance from the teacher.

Debriefing for behavioural reasons does not mean a rerun of the arguments dealt with in the simulation itself. While it is natural for the participants to have become emotionally involved and convinced of the rightness of their own particular decisions, and to say so in the debriefing, the teacher should not allow the debriefing to degenerate into a bad-tempered shouting match: 'We were right to vote for a tunnel.' 'No, you're wrong, a bridge is a much better idea.' 'Rubbish. A bridge is a stupid idea.' The actual decisions made during the simulation should be dealt with only briefly, and the debriefing should then concentrate on those aspects of the behaviour which correspond to the teacher's aims. This might be the subject matter itself – the principles and practices of the geographer, the consultant, the statesman and so forth. In a debriefing the students can compare what happened in the simulation with other possibilities, real or hypothetical, similar or dissimilar.

If the main purpose for introducing the simulation was to give practice in communication skills and decision making, then the debriefing can investigate how the decisions were arrived at. It can deal not only with what happened, but what might have happened had someone said or done something differently. It can compare the decision making in the simulation with some other model: a parliament, a committee, an army, a dictatorship, a bureaucracy.

If the teacher was aiming to demonstrate that having responsibility and power for something can be very different from the attitudes and opinions of those who are not in charge, then the debriefing can become introspective. 'I started off by thinking that it was wrong to do it, but then, after a bit, I had to look at both sides of the question. I had to do it because it was my responsibility. And then I started thinking that maybe it wasn't wrong to do it after all because...'

Introspection can occur in the debriefing of almost any simulation used for any purpose. In simulations dealing with personal and social relationships, with attitudes and prejudices, emotions, and ethical and value judgements, then the personalities of the participants may become the main topic of discussion.

Debriefing for language

There is no difference in principle between debriefing for behavioural reasons and debriefing for language reasons. In both cases the aims of the teacher can be reflected in the discussions, comments and guidance. In both cases it is a good idea to start the debriefing with the students explaining briefly what they did and why. Since the students will have been involved in the action, they will have something to talk about in a much more meaningful way than if they were discussing a film or book. The motivation involves all the students, not just those who have bright ideas. They know what they are talking about, because they are talking about what they did themselves. They are the best authority on the subject.

The debriefing can be conducted in the students' native language, or in the foreign language they are studying, or in bits of both, depending on the aims of the teacher and the circumstances. Usually, the debriefing will be in the foreign language, and will thus provide a natural continuation of the language used in the simulation.

In the language debriefing, as distinct from the behavioural debriefing, the teacher is more likely to take charge of the course of the discussion, moving from point to point, and from example to example, based on what happened (or what could or should have happened) in regard to language and communication.

Since a debriefing is usually regarded as an event which immediately follows the action, or within the next few hours, the appraisal of the language and communication skills will depend on impressions, noted down or remembered. This contrasts with a teacher's careful analysis of the words used based on a taped recording of the simulation event – a technique discussed in the next section, 'Analysing simulation discourse'. Even if, during the simulation, the Controller made a very accurate record of mistakes of grammar and pronunciation, it is unwise to devote the debriefing to a recital of mistakes. This can be very discouraging to the students, who may have felt that in practice they were communicating fairly effectively. If in the debriefing the teacher concentrates almost entirely on mistakes, then this is likely to make students reluctant to take part in future simulations, and to make them apprehensive and inhibited in their language if they do participate further. Successes should be considered as well as failures, and the language of effective communication could be dealt with as well as the mistakes of pronunciation and grammar.

Usually the teacher will have in mind specific areas for linguistic comment, which can be dealt with in a general way, using general examples. But simulations often include unexpected occurrences, and may give the teacher important insights into what the students know or do not know, and their abilities or lack of ability. So a debriefing may focus attention on a general topic, such as the differences between formal and informal speech, or else highlight a point in the action which revealed some important linguistic aspect.

It is possible for the debriefing to be conditioned by the syllabus. If the teacher expects to devote the next couple of lessons to modal auxiliaries, then in monitoring the language used during the simulation the teacher can have made notes about the use, misuse, or non-use of 'may', 'can', 'should', 'shall' and so on. These points can be made partly in the debriefing, and also partly during the subsequent lessons themselves by referring back to the simulation.

Sometimes the teacher may have no specific objective for linguistic analysis, and may simply note points at random as they arise, and use them during later lessons as convenient. While most teachers and most students would prefer that the debriefing should include comments and guidance on various aspects of language, it is not absolutely essential. Some language teachers restrict the debriefing to the sort of behavioural debriefing described earlier, and use the knowledge gained by monitoring the language as simply an indicator of the strengths and weaknesses of individual students, which can be taken into account during tuition.

Analysing simulation discourse

In addition to the more or less instantaneous debriefing for language and behaviour, the teacher may require a more thorough analysis of the conversation, debate, discussion and general discourse which occurred during the action part of the simulation. In order to do this effectively it is necessary to record the language used, and possibly produce a transcript from the recording. The result can then be analysed at leisure, free from the immediacy of the simulation event.

There are two general ways of carrying out this analysis. One is to concentrate on the words, phrases and sentences from the point of view of grammar and pronunciation. The second method, which may be more difficult, yet more appropriate, is to analyse the discourse from the point of view of functional effectiveness. The first method is straightforward, and little can be said in the way of comment or advice to the teacher; the analysis will depend on circumstances. It may consist of a list of grammatical errors and an analysis of their type and of their frequency. One category could be mistakes of pronunciation, another could be mistakes of tense, and so on. The result would produce a profile of the level of linguistic competence of the group as a whole, and individuals in particular. It would indicate to the teacher areas requiring improvement.

Here is an example of how the teacher might undertake the grammatical analysis. It comes from the transcript from a West German school where five children – who have had six years of English – are taking part in the author's *Space Crash*. One approach is to underline those errors of grammar which seem worthy of note.

```
Andro:  The information is: Dyans are friendly
        and they will show us the way to the
        radio station and there we find food      we would find
        and water. But Dyans are not drinking     do not drink
```

	water - they need only a kind of dry grass and they never move away from grassy areas.	
Erid:	Yes. Betelg?	
Betelg:	We are on a flatland. I have a compass and - er - can choose our way, but we can't go - em - diagonal on Dy. We must be careful that we do not go in circles and - em - and we can...	we diagonally
Cassi:	I know how long we can stay without water. That's three days, and - er - on Dy the valleys are not usually - usually near hills - em - and we're - er - only - nee - the only other water on Dy is at the radio station - er - that we can see the radio station - em - mast from the hill if we climb on them. And I've also the information that - em - the sand is dangerous, but I don't know why and - er - perhaps the story is untrue.	go or live or survive omit, or and hills climb up them or climb them
Draco:	I know there is a kind of - the grass - but - er - the bran, and we have to...	??
Erid:	The bran?	
Draco:	The bran - it's a sort of grass, and - em - we have to found the bran within fifteen days, and - er - and - er - we have to go at the radio station - within twenty-one days because - er - we can live with water and bran twenty days.	find get to or arrive at or reach bran for (only) twenty days
Erid:	I think it would be good if somebody notes what we're saying, or what...	
Betelg:	I have another information. It will take us about two days to reach the hill.	another bit of or another piece of
Andro:	How much?	How many? or How long?
Betelg:	Two days.	

Andro: Where's the hill?

Draco: I think it is important to reach the hill because - em - we have <u>to found</u> the radio station where the water <u>lies</u>.

<u>to find</u>

<u>is</u> or <u>is kept</u>

Andro: Ja - but we have to <u>use</u> bran because we cannot live three days without eating bran.

<u>get</u> or <u>pick</u> or <u>collect</u> or <u>eat</u>

Draco: Fifteen.

Erid: Fifteen. <u>But only</u> three days without water.

<u>But we can live</u> <u>(survive) only</u>

Cassi: We must go into the valley - because <u>there is water</u>.

<u>water is there</u> or <u>there is</u> <u>water in the</u> <u>valley</u>

Having underlined those errors of grammar which may seem significant to the teacher — and the above is merely a tentative example — the next step is to categorise the mistakes. This can be done for the whole transcript. It can also be done for individuals. On two occasions Draco says *found* instead of *find*. On the other hand, although Draco says *go at the radio station*, this may be a minor lapse as shown by the later remark *to reach the hill*. The first statement by Andro, which includes *we find* instead of *we would find*, and *are not drinking* instead of *do not drink*, indicates trouble with tenses.

The longer the transcript, the more reliable the analysis will be. The above example is only the first few minutes of the simulation, but even so it is possible to see patterns of errors emerging, and also those areas in which the participants are fluent and correct.

The second method of analysing the transcript — for communication of meaning — is a relatively new development in linguistics. There are several different approaches, but they all take into account the context of the discourse and extend the analysis beyond the sentence. Important factors are the 'cohesion' of the discourse and the knowledge which the speakers share before the discourse begins. (See Halliday's *Language as Social Semiotic* and Coulthard's *An Introduction to Discourse Analysis* as examples of this approach.) However, rather than describe the categories and the jargon of particular authors, it may be more practical for the language teacher simply to concentrate on what it is that the participants are trying to communicate. Thus, the analysis will be functional, and will depend on circumstances and context.

Here then is the *Space Crash* transcript re-analysed on the functional level of communication, context and shared knowledge. And in order to provide a sharp contrast with the earlier grammatical analysis, all the errors previously underlined are ignored, except when they impede successful communication.

The role cards of Andro, Betelg, Cassi, Draco and Erid are all different, and each has the job of explaining to the others the relevant information on the card. Part of their shared knowledge is 'Notes for Participants', which explain that they are survivors of a space crash and that it is their job to stay alive. Also part of the shared knowledge is Map Square No. 1, which is placed on the table around which they sit. They all know that they can request another map square from the Controller once they have decided which way to go, and further map squares after that, thus plotting their route across the planet.

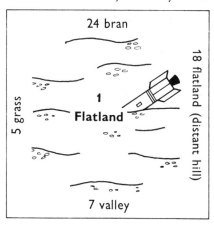

By starting 'The information is:...' Andro announces the category of the discourse; it is informational, so the listeners know what to expect before they hear the details. Unfortunately, Andro fails to mention that they have no food or water, that they have nothing to carry water in, and that they should tell the others what they know. This was due to Erid, who intervened during a gap in the explanation.

Andro: The information is: Dyans are friendly and they will show us the way to the radio station and there we find food and water. But Dyans are not drinking water – they need only a kind of dry grass and they never move away from grassy areas.

Erid decides to organise the discussion. The words have the functional meaning 'I am in charge. Thank you, Andro, for your contribution. I assume you have finished. It is now your turn, Betelg. You may begin.'

Erid: Yes. Betelg?

As an intervention it turns out to be effective, but is contrary to the interests of the group. 'Yes, Andro. Anything else?' would have been a more appropriate communication.

No one challenges Erid's self-appointed organising. Betelg fails to signpost the information and is interrupted, having been deprived of the chance to say that what is printed on the edges of the map squares is what can be seen one day's walk away, except for the distant hill, which is two days' walk away.

Betelg: We are on a flatland. I have a compass and – er – can choose our way, but we can't go – em – diagonal on Dy. We must be careful that we do not go in circles and – em – and we can...

An effective, but unhelpful interruption. 'I know how long...' is attention grabbing. It enables Cassi not only to explain how long they can survive without water, but also to pass on all the other relevant information.

Cassi: I know how long we can stay without water. That's three days and – er – on Dy the valleys are not usually – usually near hills – em – and we're – er – only – nee – the only other water on Dy is at the radio station – er – that we can see the radio station – em – mast from the hill if we climb on them. And I've also the information that – em – the sand is dangerous, but I don't know why, and – er – perhaps the story is untrue.

Like Cassi, Draco begins 'I know...', but whereas Cassi used it for signposting what was to come, Draco tries to impart the information directly, and gets into a muddle.

Draco: I know there is a kind of – the grass – but – er – the bran, and we have to...

An effective and helpful question, which guides Draco into a more efficient use of the language of explanation.	**Erid:** The bran?
Draco begins signposting: 'The bran – it's...' The noun followed by the pause, followed by the pronoun, effectively dramatises the link between the name and the description – an important point in listening to language as distinct from reading it, when 'The bran is...' would do just as well. But Draco's further information (fifteen days, twenty days, twenty-one days) has not been signposted. The following interruption deprives Draco of the opportunity to explain that bran can be easily carried and lasts for months, and to pose the question on the role card: 'How shall we decide which way to go – elect a leader, or take a vote, or what?'	**Draco:** The bran – it's a sort of grass, and – em – we have to found the bran within fifteen days, and – er – and – er – we have to go at the radio station – within twenty-one days because – er – we can live with water and bran twenty days.
Erid interrupts with a suggestion about procedure; probably in an attempt to sort out the significance of Draco's flow of facts.	**Erid:** I think it would be good if somebody notes what we're saying, or what...
The dramatic, though ungrammatical, 'I have another information' effectively silences Erid, and gives Betelg the opportunity finally to pass on the previously interrupted data. Perhaps Betelg was paying little attention to what Erid was saying, and was giving vent to a gradual build-up of emotional pressure to discharge the duty of imparting information.	**Betelg:** I have another information. It will take us about two days to reach the hill.
Also ignoring Erid's suggestion.	**Andro:** How much?

55

Betelg: Two days.

Expressing ignorance of shared knowledge. The question is answered by pointing to the words on Map Square No. 1.

Andro: Where's the hill?

Draco's statement marks a complete change of language — from the language of explanation to the language of decision making. In this case it is characterised by 'I think...'. Erid's earlier procedural suggestion also began with 'I think...', but Draco's invitation to policy language is accepted.

Draco: I think it is important to reach the hill because – em – we have to found the radio station where the water lies.

Although talking about policy, Andro again demonstrates failure to remember shared knowledge.

Andro: Ja – but we have to use bran because we cannot live three days without eating bran.

Not only precise, but brusque, probably silently communicating the admonition: 'I told you that a moment ago, and you should have remembered.'

Draco: Fifteen.

Reinforcing Draco's information; contrasting it with the three-day survival limit without water; over-bidding Draco; and continuing to say 'I am the person who is best able to organise this attempt at survival.'

Erid: Fifteen. But only three days without water.

Cassi ignores the power struggle, and concentrates on the decision making. Beginning with the categorical 'We must...', Cassi reflects not only conviction but also the importance of the choice. Although it would be less ambiguous in a literary sense if Cassi had said 'because water is there', the priority and emphasis on the word 'there' in

Cassi: We must go into the valley – because there is water.

a geographical sense justify the
transposition in speech, in contrast
to the written word.

Unlike the grammatical analysis, the above analysis of functional effectiveness is to some extent subjective. It has to be, otherwise it would not be so useful. Language is not arithmetic; it is interpreted according to context, shared knowledge and personal attitudes, and it is valuable that the interpretation should be subjective. However, the teacher can certainly discuss the interpretation with the students, either as an isolated example or as a pattern.

As with grammatical analysis, the teacher can categorise the functional effectiveness according to personal assessment of what seems interesting, important, or worth following up in future lessons. There are many avenues. One is a personal one, the different use of techniques: signposting, questioning and categorical statements by individuals. Another is a general approach, for example, the variety of forms of question: 'Betelg?' 'The bran?' 'Where is the hill?' Whereas the last is a specific request for specific information, the first is more a request, or an order, than a question, even though the intonation is that of a question. The difference between the spoken and written word is also a useful line of enquiry.

The contextual appropriateness of the discourse is another fruitful field. Despite the need for shared knowledge, nobody said 'Have you told us everything?' There was little defence against interruption; no one said 'I have three important points for survival – firstly...' Some participants used preliminary signposting effectively. Others failed to sort out what they wanted to say.

Even in the above analysis, which occupied only the first few minutes of the simulation, certain patterns of language, attitudes, abilities and character begin to emerge. Clearly, the longer the extract, the more reliable the conclusions. Also, the more varied the simulation, the more varied the discourse will be. The transcript of a simulation about management – trade union negotiations will have different characteristics from that of a public inquiry, where witnesses give evidence and are questioned.

Analysis of simulation discourse differs markedly from analysis of ordinary classroom talk, where the teacher is in control of the discussion. The seminal *Towards an Analysis of Discourse* by Sinclair and Coulthard is based entirely on teacher – pupil talk. The reason was to make it easier to examine the structure of the discourse in a lesson than in, say, casual conversation. Certainly, it did reveal plenty of interruptions by the teachers to guide the discussion down pre-prepared paths, which were not clearly revealed in advance to the pupils. In many cases the discourse was question and answer. The motives of the children seemed to be 'What is it that the teacher wishes me to say?' rather than 'How can I contribute usefully to the discussion?' Sinclair and Coulthard also noticed what they describe as 'frames' – transactional discourse separated by frames which were often clearly marked by the teacher saying 'yes', 'good', 'right', 'now' and so on. It was part of the shared knowledge between teacher and pupils that these words did not have their normal meanings. The words 'good' and 'yes' were not usually commendations, but signals for changing the topic or advancing the same topic one stage further. They marked the end of one transaction, and signalled the beginning of the next. In simulation discourse, the cohesion of the discussion does not lie in any kind of teacher intervention; it arises naturally and spontaneously out of the context, functions, duties and responsibilities. And as such, it is just as easy (if not easier) to analyse as trying to analyse the intentions, understandings and misunderstandings in teacher–pupil discourse.

The two types of analysis – grammatical and functional – are not mutually exclusive. As demonstrated above, the same transcript can be used for both. The two complement each other. Occasionally, of course, there may be a divergent judgement between the grammatical and the functional. The sentence 'I have another information' can be functionally effective, despite being grammatically incorrect. Similarly, there are examples of sentences which are grammatically correct but fail to achieve their functional objective. Both grammatical and functional analyses of simulation discourse help the teacher to construct profiles of the students, whether as a class, or as individuals, indicating strengths and weaknesses. These profiles can then be used, not only for discussion with the students, but also as a guide to making future lessons more effective.

Whatever happened to Erid?

The detailed analysis of the *Space Crash* transcript stopped at the point where the language was changing from the language of explanation to the language of decision making. Since the reader may be curious to know what happened next, and since the aim of the book is to encourage teachers to get inside the simulation experience, it may be valuable to give the rest of the transcript. This is reproduced without comments so that individual teachers can envisage the event as occurring in their own classroom and in relation to their own aims and syllabus, and can use the transcript as raw material for their own analysis of discourse.

The map squares which were requested by the participants and handed over by the Controller are reproduced alongside the text in order to provide the context of shared knowledge. What is missing, of course, is the physical behaviour – the gestures, pointing at aspects of the map squares, the facial expressions and tones of voice. These will have to be imagined. The transcript continues where it left off, with Cassi advocating travel to the valley.

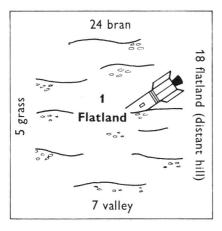

Cassi: We must go into the valley –
because there is water.
Betelg: I understand that radio station
– that there is water, too.
Andro: The Dyans live in the grassland
– where the grass is, there must
be water.
Draco: No – er – the grass –
Erid: Needs no water.
Draco: Yes.
Andro: The Dyans can show us the
radio station.
Erid: But at first we have to go to the
valley, I think.
Betelg: You are the Controller.
(*laughter*)
Cassi: Let's go to the water.
Draco: I think so – number 7.
Andro: OK.

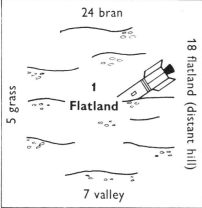

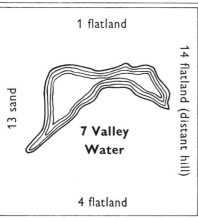

Andro: Valley. Schreib auf. (*Write it
down.*)
Draco: Water.
Erid: Now we have water.
Betelg: But there is nothing to carry it in.
(*laughter*)
Draco: Perhaps we drink and then we go
to the decent – er – distant hill
because it's two days to reach
the hill and we can stay three
days without water and from
the hills we can see the radio
station.
Erid: OK.
Betelg: We can see only...
Andro: Wir haben jetzt Wasser. (*Now
we have some water.*)
Erid: In English.
Betelg: But we've nothing to eat.
Draco: We can stay fifteen days without
eating.
Erid: So it's not so important.
Cassi: OK. Number 14.

The follow-up

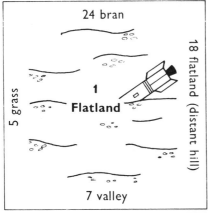

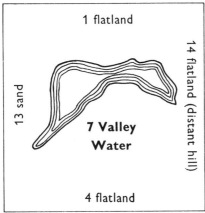

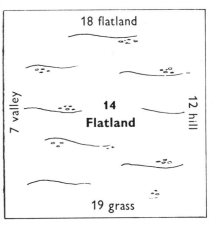

Cassi: There are hills.
Draco: We have to go two days...
Betelg: We have to go...
Andro: To the grass.
Betelg: This is one day to the grass.
Cassi: We can't eat the grass.
Erid: Can we eat it or not?
Cassi: No.
Andro: Near the grass are the Dyans.
Erid: Yes?
Andro: Yes. Dann könn' wir ja erst so gehen und dann... (*laughter*) (*First we can go this way, and then...*)
Erid: And what's in the flatland?
Cassi: In the flatland?
Erid: Has someone got any information? The flatland?
Cassi: Which flatland?

Draco: But when we go to the hill it's two days and back is one day and water is here.
Betelg: Yes, we have no water there.
Andro: We've first to go to the grass here.
Erid: Why that?
Andro: There are living the Dyans.
Draco: But they haven't also no water.
Betelg: They don't drink any water.
Andro: But they can show us the water.
Cassi: Yes.
Andro: We go to the grass.
Erid: We go − there?
Cassi: Yes.
Erid: Which number is it?
Andro: Nineteen.

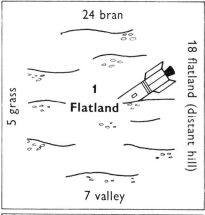

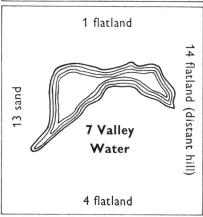

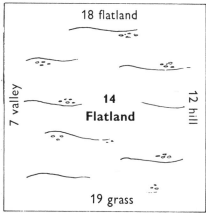

Erid: Grass and no Dyans.
(?) Aaahhhh.
Cassi: Sand...sand...
Draco: Tooot.
Andro: We go to the hills.
Erid: I think...
Betelg: We go back to the water.
Draco: Yes, yes, that's our only chance.
Erid: Yes, and then?
Andro: Why not the hill?
Erid: And then?
Andro: Back to the flatland.
Betelg: No, no − sand.
Cassi: Sand is dangerous.
Andro: All right.
Erid: Flatland; flatland; flatland.
Cassi: Back to there.
Erid: There we're dead.

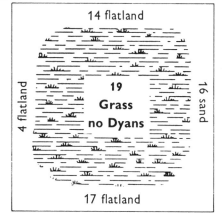

61

Betelg: But now...
Andro: I think we have to go to the hill.
Erid: Then we are dead — we can't go back.
(?) — hmmm —
Draco: Perhaps when we went to the flatland, and then to the grass, and now there's no water, and...
Betelg: We're dead.
Erid: Right.
Draco: And it's the same if we go to the hill and then we go back.
Andro: We could have gone there (*pointing at bran*) the first day...

Erid has a diary showing that it is the second day without water. Since no diagonal movements are allowed, the space crew have realised that death is inevitable — they cannot reach water on the third day. The language is spontaneously changing from the language of decision making to the language of inquest: 'We could have...' 'We should have...' 'If we had...'

In the classroom the Controller and participants may wish to continue the action. And since there are forty-one map squares and a long way to go to the radio station, the Controller usually retrieves the last map square, saying, in this case, 'You have gone back one day. It is still the second day without water and you are on flatland, square number 14.' Sometimes the Controller makes it a condition that they read their role cards again, as they may have omitted to pass on some vital piece of information. Death was salutary; it demonstrated that the Controller does not intervene in decision making.

Follow-up activities

Simulations are often characterised by creative follow-up activities. The emotional involvement and the mind-jogging nature of simulations provoke ideas from both participants and Controller.

Sometimes the idea is to 'look at the real thing'. If the class has participated in a newspaper simulation, they may wish to visit the offices of a real newspaper; if it was a business simulation, they may want to visit the offices of a real company. As well as visiting, the participants may also wish to do something — start up a class newspaper or radio programme, run a classroom company to manufacture cardboard lapel badges or organise the accounts of the social club. It is not unusual for students to propose the devising of educational activities to follow up certain aspects of a simulation experience — project work, role-play exercises, games, informal drama and so forth. Sometimes students want to try their hand at writing their own educational follow-up activities. Simulations can arouse interest in areas which would otherwise receive little or no attention — from the rock drawings of American Indians to the psychology of group dynamics.

The language and communication aspect of the simulation is likely to receive particular attention. It provides a focus and a motive for ideas. Since simulations, by their nature, emphasise language for action, it is likely that most suggestions will be in this area. Experience with the simulation technique will help the teacher make some useful predictions about the sort of students who are likely to come up with useful ideas, and the probable nature of these follow-up activities. Even so, some useful ideas are unpredictable.

The creative ideas which often follow a good simulation provide another reason why the teacher, and the syllabus planner, should try to have flexible options in the periods after a simulation. It is not only that the ideas themselves can be educationally beneficial, but that the willingness to provide opportunities for trying out such ideas can increase student motivation. The follow-up activities can thus be regarded as part of the educational philosophy which embraces the simulation technique: that students should be encouraged to be active participants in the learning process.

6 Will the simulation work?

Dissecting a simulation

The way in which language can be used in a simulation depends largely upon the structure and mechanics of the simulation. So, in order that the teacher can make the best use of simulations for language purposes, it is desirable to know something about simulation design – about the nitty-gritty, the devices, the options and the categories. It is valuable to be able to spot a simulation in the way that an expert can spot the various types of aircraft, cars, or railway engines. Even the knowledge of what makes one different from another, and what combination of features is dangerous, can make all the difference between a simulation which is used successfully for language purposes, and one which is a flop.

One category is whether the simulation is open-ended or closed. A closed simulation has a 'right' answer. In general – and there are quite a few exceptions – the language in closed simulations tends to be precise and analytical, concerned with facts and the verifiable results of altering these facts. Many business simulations possess these characteristics, with concrete variables, such as output, costs and advertising. Sometimes what would ordinarily be an open-ended simulation is transformed into a closed one by introducing scoring mechanisms which are not inherent in the simulated environment. In a simulation about voting in a legislature the number of votes cast for and against a proposition is inherent; but to arbitrarily award ten marks to any member who successfully raises a point of order is not inherent. American simulations sometimes tend towards non-inherent scoring mechanisms in order to enable the teacher to test the objective validity of the learning and perhaps to increase motivation. However, this is a design fault. It damages plausibility and reality of function, and introduces gaming motivation. From the language point of view it is undesirable, since the language becomes less authentic. If the language of gaming is the objective, then it is better to use a genuine game for that purpose.

Open-ended simulations have no 'right' answer. They can have several answers or it can be a situation in which 'answer' is an unsuitable word to describe what the participants are trying to achieve. In general – and again there are exceptions – the language in an open-ended simulation is likely to be wider in scope and purpose than in a closed simulation.

Interaction is another important criterion of classification. At one extreme are non-interactive simulations. The interaction is the interaction of the hermit or the dictator taking solitary decisions in response to the environment, documents, and possibly the equipment. However, the number of participants is not a measure of the degree of interaction, since it is quite possible for the participants to spend most of their time divided up and working on their own. Participation is determined by the mechanics – who has to do what, and with what help (or hindrance) from whom? Some simulations have part-time roles or functions, or passive functions. A jury in a simulation of a trial could go through the whole simulation and say very little indeed. Other simulations are fully participatory, giving everyone an equal opportunity, and perhaps having built-in provisions for each participant to say something. Other things being equal, a fully participatory simulation is likely to be a good one for language purposes.

Some simulations are imaginative, mind-jogging and inspiring; others are routine and pedestrian. Depending on the aims of the Controller, either type could be desirable for language purposes. But there is no doubt that different sorts of language occur in the two types – imaginative and non-imaginative. The non-imaginative is likely to be useful for practising forms of speech which are routine transactions, whereas the imaginative type of simulation encourages speculation, analogies and invention. Creative thoughts can result in creative language. So when looking at simulation material, the Controller should ask the question: what are the tasks, the resources and the options?

Another useful category to bear in mind is whether the simulation is consistent within itself, or whether it contains inconsistencies of aims and motives. If, in an otherwise genuine simulation, a role card invites a participant to play-act, then that is an inconsistency. This affects the mechanics of the simulation, the motives and the language. If a simulation includes events which are normally the results of chance – such as the weather on a particular day, or the number of soldiers killed in a rocket attack – then it is consistent to determine this by chance mechanisms: a dice, chance cards and so on. But if chance cards, or dice, are introduced to determine what would normally be decided by discussion and decision making, then this reduces plausibility, damages reality of function, and introduces a superfluous gaming element. All these are likely to affect the behaviour, motives and language of the participants. The language is likely to become more detached from functional decision making, and more concerned with appraising the results of the turn of the card. Diminished participant responsibility can lead to discussions about the chance mechanisms themselves ('Whose turn is it?' 'Throw the dice.' 'Let's turn over another chance card.' 'I've won.') rather than thinking and talking about duties, responsibilities, problems and decisions.

The following two simulations have been chosen as examples from the short list of recommended simulations in Chapter 2. They differ in many ways. *Talking Rocks* is simple, short, yet mind-jogging. The participants cannot call on their previous experiences to help them. All are equal: the teenager and the professor; the man and the woman; the immigrant and the native.

The amount of reading to be done before the action starts is virtually nil. The opportunities for fully participatory interaction are many. By contrast, *North Sea Challenge* is long, is based on analysis of facts and figures, and has many documents. The mechanics of the first and last stage – *Strike* and *Impact* – are fairly routine, but the second stage, *Slick*, is novel and imaginative. The degree of authenticity of the documentation is excellent, but there are unnecessary inconsistencies in the design of the simulation. Although *North Sea Challenge* is far more expensive than *Talking Rocks*, both, in their way, are good value for money.

Both simulations are described in some detail so as to enable the reader to spot the categories, and to ascertain the sort of classroom situation which would be suitable for each. A key point to watch for is the likely influence of the mechanisms and structures of the simulations on the sort of language, behaviour, and communicative and social skills which are likely to occur.

Talking Rocks

Talking Rocks is a survival simulation, but it is very different from either *Space Crash* or *Humanus*. It concerns the 'Eagle people', prehistoric shepherds who live in groups and seasonally migrate in search of new pastures. The Eagle people communicate with each other by leaving messages (on rocks) near abandoned camp sites giving vital information about how to survive. But although the nomadic shepherds speak the same language, they have no written language, no alphabet and no system of numbers. Obviously, the aim is not to teach students to become prehistoric shepherds. Subject-based pigeon holes are not particularly suitable for categorising simulations. Nor is the author's aim always a reliable guide. What matters is what happens in the event.

In the case of *Talking Rocks*, the author is an American, Robert F. Vernon, who had made a study of prehistoric cave drawings, and travelled with his wife in many areas to collect materials and evidence on the subject. In the teacher's manual, Vernon intimates that the main aim (and perhaps the original aim) is to attack the stereotypes of 'primitive people' and 'noble savages', and instead to come to appreciate just how sophisticated, ingenious and talented our early ancestors were. But with this aim, the simulation could have been completely different in its mechanism. It could have been based on a department of anthropology, where participants discussed evidence and theories about petroglyphs and pictographs. Instead, there is no looking back into prehistory; the participants are in prehistory. If anyone is sophisticated and ingenious, then it is the participants themselves. Survival is not a fact for comment; it is an aim to be achieved by the participants. It is probably significant that *Talking Rocks* was published by Garry Shirts' company, Simile II, and that Vernon, in the introduction, pays tribute to the good advice and criticism which he received from simulation experts. The mind-jogging element is for the participant to be placed in the prehistoric hot seat, and this is the vital mechanical factor which influences the language used.

The situation, as explained in the briefing, is this: the participants are to be divided into groups, each representing a band of Eagle people, and the bands are located at camp sites as far away from each other as the geography of the classroom will allow. Each camp site has an easel (or board) with large sheets of paper for drawing the survival messages, so positioned that they are not observable from other camp sites. The camp sites are supposed to be separated by journeys of many days over high plateaux and arid deserts.

The Controller explains that the bands move simultaneously from one camp site to the next one and supposedly never meet each other; so if they bump into each other when moving in the restricted area of the classroom, they must not talk to each other. Similarly, there is a restriction on talking which is loud enough to be overheard by the band at another camp site. What they do when they arrive at an abandoned camp site is to try to make sense of the message left by the previous band, and then to write their own message based on the information in a card handed out by the Controller. The manual contains a diagram showing how the classroom furniture could be arranged to accommodate five camp sites, and there are twelve survival messages which are gradually handed out by the Controller. Message number 6 is as follows:

SURVIVAL MESSAGE

Travel south across the desert from here for two days. You will find a river. Follow the river to the west for half a day and you will find a huge pasture.

The reverse side of the messages all contain the following instructions, which reinforce the instructions given by the Controller.

(1) No talking between bands at any time.
(2) Keep this message a secret.
(3) Use only pictures to write the message.

There is a ban on modern signs, symbols and numbers. Participants cannot, for example, use the skull and crossbones sign to indicate poison, or use the letters (or words) representing the points of the compass.

The manual is excellently written, covering almost all the points which are relevant to the smooth running of the simulation. One point not mentioned, however, is the fact that the bands who survive are not always the most ingenious. 'You're alive because we left you our good message. We're dead because we could not make sense of your ambiguous message.' This is the sort of thing that can happen in a simulation, and it is useful for the Controller to envisage what could go wrong, and how to deal with it. The Controller, in this case, can wait till the resentment occurs and then say 'That's how life is sometimes. But at least the knowledge of the good symbols will help the whole of the Eagle people to survive, and the knowledge that you died because of the poor symbols will help the others to improve their skills. Besides, death is not permanent, and you can re-enter the simulation.' Alternatively, the resentment might be prevented by explaining the situation in the briefing.

Suggestions for the debriefing and follow-up are shorter, yet more imaginative and more consistent, than those in *North Sea Challenge*. Vernon says he was inspired by the advice on debriefing from a well-known simulation expert, Ron Stadsklev. Unfortunately, Vernon seems to have imported Stadsklev's terminology into this section, and whereas the first part of the manual refers to the activity as a simulation, the debriefing section refers to it as a game. This could be dangerous, as indicated elsewhere in this book. If the Controller describes it as a game, or uses gaming language, then gaming behaviour is likely to ensue, with participants trying to 'win' by staying alive, and perhaps sabotaging their own drawings in order to make another group 'lose'. The gaming element can result in cheating; it can cause play-acting and the brandishing of 'spears' as groups pass each other. The language can become that of humour or protest rather than survival, duty and function.

In *Talking Rocks*, as in *Space Crash*, the form of the discourse is informal, exploratory, and requires imaginative decision making. Both simulations involve a leap away from day-to-day experiences. Consequently, the behaviour and the language used may surprise the Controller – and the participants themselves – since it will not involve the teacher–student hierarchy of more customary classroom discourse. The debriefing also is likely to be more wide-ranging and unpredictable than in *North Sea Challenge*. It can relate to grammar. The drawing of a sheep can represent nouns, verbs, adverbs and adjectives. A fat sheep can represent good pasture, a thin sheep can be poor pasture. A group of sheep walking towards a hill can mean 'Go in this direction', and so on. Comparisons in the way different bands draw the same message can be used to illustrate points about the development of language, and the use of a writing system. What usually happens in the simulation is that after several migrations from camp to camp an accepted writing pattern begins to emerge, with groups accepting and copying useful ideas, and abandoning the misleading or erroneous symbols. It becomes clear that the aim is not to reproduce reality, but to use pictures to convey meaning.

Like *Space Crash*, the relevance of *Talking Rocks* to the language classroom is not to be found in classifying it as 'survival', or 'futurology', or 'pre-history'. Those are subject areas, and the teacher should try to get behind the label and find out what actually happens in the event itself, and judge the simulation accordingly.

North Sea Challenge

Whereas *Talking Rocks* consists of a 24-page teacher's manual incorporating survival messages, *North Sea Challenge* weighs two kilograms: there are dozens of data cards, facsimile documents, two cassette tapes, a film strip and a large, glossy teacher's guide. It is produced by BP Educational Service.

The mechanics consist of three separate but interrelated simulations, entitled *Strike*, *Slick* and *Impact*, all concerned with the fictitious oil company, Norsoco, and all dealing with problems located on the east coast of Scotland, and offshore. Place names are a mixture of the real and the fictitious. It might have been better to rely entirely on fictitious geography, perhaps by turning the map 90 degrees, which would have given the simulation a somewhat greater degree of universality, but this is a small point. The geography is essential to the action in all three simulations.

STRIKE

The class is divided into groups, each group taking on the identity of one person – Mr W. Stewart of Norsoco's Engineering Division, Aberdeen – who has the task of investigating alternative ways of producing and transporting crude oil ashore.

SLICK

The class is divided into groups, each group taking on the identity of the Local Pollution Officer, Mr A. McTaggart, in the (fictitious) Scottish port of Inverlochen. Mr McTaggart has the job of drawing up a contingency plan for dealing with an oil slick, and then has the job of dealing with the slick when it occurs. A cassette recording gives intermittent information about wind speed and direction; and this affects the movement of the oil slick.

IMPACT

The class is divided into four groups representing the oil company, the District Council, the residents of Inverlochen, and the residents of Stomar. It is the job of these four groups to represent their own interests at a public debate on whether an oil terminal should be sited at Inverlochen or Stomar (or neither).

All three simulations include data cards, which can be requested from the Controller by any group wishing to explore a specific aspect of the problem. For example, in *Slick* there are six data cards: 1 Absorption, 2 Sinking, 3 Dispersant, 4 Booms, 5 Oil on the shore, 6 Behaviour of oil at sea. In addition there are very authentic-looking letters, maps and so on, which are handed out to each group at the start of the simulation.

In *Slick*, one of the documents common to all groups is the letter to the Local Pollution Officer, Mr A. McTaggart, from Norsoco's Environmental Control Manager. (see p. 71)

In *Impact*, some of the documents are confidential to individual groups. The Norsoco team, for example, has an internal Norsoco memo from M.R. Haynes to the Public Relations Officer, and no other group receives a copy of this document. (see p. 72)

Also in *Impact*, the residents of the two towns have role cards, but not the Norsoco team, nor the representatives of the District Council. The role cards are confidential, and each consists of four or five sentences explaining who they are and why they object to having an oil terminal constructed on their doorsteps, or why they would welcome such a development. One of the female members of the Stomar residents' group is J. Morton. This is her role card:

J. Morton

If God had wanted us to have North Sea oil he wouldn't have put it at the bottom of the North Sea. That's your opinion and you are very angry about the proposed development. Your husband was buried in the cemetery near the proposed site and you believe it's a sacrilege that English oil companies should be exploiting Scottish oil and trampling all over the countryside ruining the local amenities. They'll all be gone when they've got all their money anyway.

Head office: Norsoco House, Park Lane, London W1A 1AA. Tel 01 920 1212

Module 2

Our reference	Your reference	Telephone	Date
BJ/PT		ext 415	3rd July

Mr A McTaggart
Local Pollution Officer
Northsand View
Inverlochen

Dear Mr McTaggart

Congratulations on your new appointment as Local Pollution Officer for Inverlochen.

In response to your request at last week's meeting of the Local Environment Advisory Committee, I enclose a map which you might find helpful in drawing up your own oil spill contingency plans. This map also shows speed and direction of local currents which will help you to plot the path of an oil slick in the event of a spill.

As your section of the coast is particularly vulnerable, it would be advisable to formulate immediate plans to combat a limited oil spill. I understand you have a budget of £5000 and you are planning to be able to deal with a spill of up to 100 tonnes.

As a main method you should choose just <u>one</u> of the following: absorbing, sinking, dispersing, or burning.

You should also examine the possibilities of dealing with oil on the shore and using a boom as a barrier.

Yours sincerely

B J Reynolds
Environmental Control Manager

Project Manager (UK)
Telex No: London 68871
Inland telegrams
Norsoco Ldn

Norsoco Ltd
Registered office:
Registered in
England
No: 1024986

B3.4

Norsoco Briefing

Module 3

NORSOCO IMPACT!

MEMO

TO: ..Public Relations Officer......

FROM: ....M R Haynes..........

DATE: ....3rd March..........

Please find enclosed map which show the two alternative sites which the company have been investigating with a view to establishing a steel platform construction yard.

Objections to the proposal have been lodged from both towns. There will be a public debate at Stomar town hall later this month. You will present the company's choice (Inverlochen), answer questions from residents, generally test the mood of the local people and, within limits, make certain compensatory offers. We would be quite generous in this.

I don't need to tell you that this is a sensitive area and we must tread carefully. You should, however, stress quite forcefully that in the race to get the oil ashore as quickly as possible production platforms are urgently required and the installation of such sites as we propose is in the national interest.

PROPOSED SITES

1. Inverlochen

Advantages

- flat land available
- land adjacent to deep water
- suitable deep channel to open sea
- suitable site for jetty construction
- adequate distance from town but close for services
- disused aerodrome and railway in vicinity (could possibly be renovated for movement of personnel etc)
- some local labour available

Disadvantages

- environmentally sensitive area (particularly wild fowl)
- close to holiday beaches
- strong opposition from local people
- need for special housing facilities etc
- possible disturbance to lobster and crab fisheries

2. Stomar

Advantages

- flat land available
- existing harbour facilities (in decay)
- close to town
- local labour available

Disadvantages

- need for dredging to deepen channel
- large-scale improvement to harbour necessary
- some housing facilities necessary
- no railway
- some local opposition

The author of *North Sea Challenge*, Michael Lynch of Bath University School of Education, spent many months researching the information, visiting oil platform sites, meeting conservationists, geologists and others. Consequently, the simulation contains a great deal of highly detailed and authentic information. To choose *North Sea Challenge* for class use is to make a considerable investment of class time and money, and it is important for the teacher to ask the question – 'Will it work?' And if there are faults in the design of the simulation, the terminology and the mechanics, can the teacher do anything to stop the ship running onto the rocks?

The first step could be to compare the teacher's guide with the documents and see if they are consistent. The introduction to the guide says: '*North Sea Challenge* has one main aim: to enable students to participate in the experience of decision making.' If the language teacher agrees with this aim, then the documents can be examined one after the other to see if they maximise decision-making opportunities, and whether the instructions in the guide are helpful in this respect. If they are muddled or inconsistent when presented by the Controller, then not only will the simulation not run smoothly, but instead of the language being the language of decision making, it can degenerate into the language of procedural queries: 'Can we do this?' 'Are we all supposed to be one person?' 'Can we take decisions, or do we have to simply list the options?'

One problem is that the guide talks in terms of case studies. All three activities are labelled case studies. In the instructions for *Strike* and *Slick* there is no mention of the allocation of roles, and the instructions suggest a case-study approach, with the groups looking at the problems from the outside. If the Controller decides to follow this procedure, then the participants are one step away from participating in decision making; they are simply taking a detached view and expressing opinions about the suitability of options. The language becomes the language of observers ('What the company might do is...') rather than the language of decision-making action ('What we should do is...').

Unlike the guide, the documents themselves invite participation in decision making. In *Slick*, for example, the drawing up of the contingency plans and the actual orders to deal with the slick as it grows in size and sweeps towards the shore are seen from the viewpoint of Mr A. McTaggart. But to have everyone in the role of a clone of Mr McTaggart diminishes plausibility, decision making and reality of function. In this case the Controller can say 'John is Mr McTaggart, and the rest of you are his staff', which establishes a leadership situation; or else 'Mr McTaggart has gone sick; you are all his assistants and have to take joint responsibility for the decision making.'

Impact is certainly not a case study, since everyone is inside the event, and roles are allocated. Unfortunately, not all the roles are based on function. Ms J. Morton is invited to play-act, and invent arguments about theology, since at the public debate she will be expected to say more than the few sentences on the role card. The personality she is given precludes arguing a rational case; she is cast in the part of an emotional protester who is 'very angry', and when she has her turn upon the stage, can be expected to act out the part, and perhaps shout abuse, and if the acting is really dramatic, can be carried screaming from the meeting. This can be fine informal drama, but it is not a simulation, and in practice can lead to acting and overacting from other participants who feel that their intellectual analysis is being upstaged by actors and actresses. Not only will the language change within the simulation, but participants may start stepping outside the simulation by abandoning reality of function, or accusing other participants of inventing 'facts', and so on. To prevent such occurrences, the Controller would be well advised to remove such role cards, and substitute them with a personal or group identity which does allow rational argument and realistic decision making.

But undoubtedly the least satisfactory role is that of the group representing Norsoco's Public Relations Officer. Such a person would be an unlikely representative of the company at a meeting where the company's plans are certain to be attacked by the people whose lives will be affected by the decisions. The role(s) should be of executive and managerial status – the chairman or deputy chairman might be appropriate – but not someone who could be regarded as a 'non-decision-making smoothie'.

Even worse is the fact of built-in duplicity. The Norsoco Company has organised the meeting and the advertising poster says that the 'sites are under consideration'. This gives the impression that it is an open question, ripe for decision making. But as the Norsoco memo explains, the decision has already been made – the company's choice is Inverlochen. Not only is the Public Relations Officer group prevented from deciding this question by weighing up the various advantages and disadvantages of the two sites, but they are not told the reason for the particular choice. ('And who is this M.R. Haynes, anyway?') If any question is likely at the meeting, it is 'Why Inverlochen?' The group can make a guess (trouble later from head office if they do), or else say 'Sorry, the company have not told us why Inverlochen has been chosen.' This is hardly the mechanism for participation in decision making.

The teacher's guide asks the Controller to give a secret briefing to the Norsoco team, instructing them not to reveal that Inverlochen has been chosen until well into the debate. The Controller tells them to start the meeting by presenting 'a balanced case for development in the region. The Norsoco group should not reveal their preference for the Inverlochen site at this early stage of the debate.' This device is known in simulation literature as a 'hidden agenda'. Usually there is a very good reason for it; but in this case it seems nonsensical. It reduces still further the decision-making powers of the Norsoco group, and it leaves them open to the charge of dishonesty. 'Why didn't you tell us when the meeting began that you'd already chosen Inverlochen?' Perhaps, in the circumstances, the best reply would be to step outside the simulation and say 'Sorry about that. We know it is deceitful, but the Controller told us we must do it that way.' The worst reply would be to stammer ineffectually, and then spend the next few coffee-shop sessions articulately criticising the Controller.

The Haynes memo is a good example of the sort of thing which the Controller should look for in deciding whether or not a simulation will work. The language is wrong for decision making: 'You will present the company's choice (Inverlochen), answer questions from residents, generally test the mood of the local people, and, within limits, make certain compensatory offers.' The phrase 'You will present...' places the participants in an inferior position. The responsibility for answering questions without knowing the answers places them in an impossible position. The instruction 'generally test the mood' is meaningless without some guidance about how they are to do this. The reference to 'within limits, make certain compensatory offers' is tantalisingly vague. What limits? What are the types of offer that can be made? Either the participants press on and hope for the best, or else they start asking questions of the Controller: 'Can we telephone head office to clarify this memo?' What does the Controller reply? To say 'No' is implausible and unsatisfactory, and to say 'Yes' means that the Controller may have to try to unravel and perhaps rewrite the memo in the middle of the simulation at the expense of monitoring the general behaviour, language and communication skills.

Consequently, it is better to anticipate problems and try to prevent them arising. In this case, the Haynes memo could be quietly left in the pack, and another one substituted which confers decision-making powers, leaves open the choice, and lists the advantages and disadvantages. The hidden agenda can also be safely ignored. The participants of all four teams can be asked to make their own decisions and behave as best they can in the circumstances in which they find themselves. Role cards which invite acting can be removed. The public meeting can be changed to a public inquiry, with a role or roles for a government inspector, and the inquiry can thus have the final say in whether the company should be permitted to build the terminal at the site they propose, whichever that might be.

These suggestions for adapting the simulation — and the reader may think of better ways of doing this — entail an hour or two of extra work in preparing the simulation materials for use. But since it is an important and long simulation, with considerable benefits in authenticity, the extra trouble and effort involved may well be a small price to pay for useful decision-making language practice.

7 Assessing the result

Validity of the simulation technique

In the 1950s and 1960s, when the simulation technique was finding its way into classrooms, there was much talk about validity. The pioneers of simulations, who were often faced with scepticism, were naturally anxious to justify simulations. There were many experiments, most of them on a small scale. Some had limited objectives and conclusions: 'This particular simulation seems to work with these students in these circumstances for these reasons.' Others were more ambitious, and sought to establish that the simulation technique was superior to alternative methods of teaching. Both types of experiment tended to reveal what any experienced user of simulations knows: that simulations are likely to produce a high level of motivation; that they are popular with students and teachers; and that most participants are convinced that simulation experiences are educationally valuable, even though such gains may not be measurable by objective tests.

Attempts to establish objectively a superiority for the simulation technique compared with other techniques failed. The reason was not because the research results were not encouraging, but because it was not a research question. It concerned value judgements. No amount of research could rank techniques in order of educational value, producing a list showing the relative educational merits of the lecture compared with the textbook, the discussion, the informal drama and so on. Not only does the answer depend on educational values, and these vary from teacher to teacher, but the question of the comparison of techniques is without meaning unless the circumstances are considered.

Validity of the simulation technique is an important question, but it is an empirical one, and one for language teachers and course planners to decide. The question is this: in these circumstances, with these aims, with these students and with this choice of materials, which technique or combination of techniques is likely to be the most effective?

The investigations of the simulation pioneers helped to draw attention to the simulation technique and to establish its credibility in the eyes of educationalists. Most of the pioneers had a chapter on assessment in their books, but unfortunately it was devoted entirely to the question of people testing simulations. The idea that simulations could test people did not seem to have been considered. Yet for the language teacher, this is the most important aspect of assessment. How valid is the simulation technique as a tool of assessment? Outside the educational field – in industry and in the armed forces – simulations have long been used as an assessment tool. In education generally, simulations are now fairly well established as a tool for learning. The time seems to be ripe for extending their use into the area of assessment. There is plenty of scope for this, particularly in the field of language assessment.

The question 'Can simulations help assessment in language learning?' is an important one. It is a question which should be asked by examination boards, inspectors, curriculum planners, tutors and teachers.

Aims and tools

In all forms of assessment, the tools should be appropriate to the aims of the assessors. Pencil and paper assessment is appropriate for most forms of knowledge testing – whether of mathematics, history, or irregular verbs. But if the aim is to assess behavioural skills – driving a car, television or radio sports commentating, portrait painting, or oral communication skills – then some form of behavioural assessment is appropriate.

There are other questions to be considered: the particular test to be used; whether the scoring is objective or subjective; the training of assessors; the cost of the testing, and so on. But these are secondary issues, which should not obscure the answer to the main question – is the assessment tool appropriate to the aim of the assessors?

It was the gap between the aim and the assessment result which was the main reason for the introduction of simulations for assessment. One of the earliest examples of the systematic use of simulations was in the Prussian Army at about the turn of the century. It came about through dissatisfaction with the inefficiency of traditional pencil and paper tests plus an interview. Too many of the wrong sort of officers were being selected, and not enough of the right sort. The solution was to introduce behavioural tests. Although details of the types of simulation which were used for the testing are lacking, they were presumably specifically designed to assess those skills and qualities which were regarded as important for the job.

Spies, managers and civil servants

The Prussian experience was followed by a similar development in the British Army, which is now regarded as a leading pioneer in the use of simulations for assessment. The types which are used vary widely. There are TEWTs (Tactical Exercise Without Troops), in which command decisions are made at 'staff headquarters'. Although there are no troops and no bullets, there is reality of function in the analysis of intelligence reports and in the battle strategies and tactics. There are simulations which test ingenuity, patience and leadership: as when a group has to move a crate of high explosives (heavy box) across a raging torrent (stream) with no special equipment apart from what can be found on the site – a few planks which are not long enough, some rope, a couple of empty oil drums, and so on.

During the Second World War the Americans had a problem about how to recruit suitable agents and spies for the OSS (Office of Strategic Services). Traditional selection procedures had been unsatisfactory, and this state of affairs might have continued had it not been for several disasters, including one in Italy where American criminals had been recruited in the mistaken belief that a dirty job requires dirty men to do it. At that time an OSS officer returned from London and described how simulations were used for the purposes of selection and training in the British Army. This solution to the problem was accepted by the Americans, who set up various centres for assessing candidates for the OSS. This included one centre which had a three-day course of simulations, exercises and improvisations. The whole course was a simulation, since each candidate had to invent and maintain a cover story about his identity and background, and maintain this throughout the course, despite attempts by members of the staff to trap candidates into revealing their true identity and background.

These courses (OSS 1948) were run mainly by officers and psychiatrists. Some of the experiences produced theoretical concepts which are relevant to education. For example, it was agreed that pencil and paper tests should constitute only part of the measures of intelligence. The concept of 'practical intelligence' was developed, later to be renamed 'effective intelligence'. This meant that if an assessor made a judgement about a candidate's intelligence based only on pencil and paper tests, then this could be legitimately disputed by observers who had witnessed the candidate's 'effective intelligence' in behavioural tests.

Partly as a result of this OSS experience, the simulation technique was developed after the war as a tool of assessment in business management in the United States. As pointed out by J.L. Moses (1977): 'In retrospect, it seems quite apparent that the procedures used for identifying a successful spy by the OSS, for example, bear a close relationship to the kind of procedures used to identify a successful manager.' All that was needed was to analyse the function and then produce the appropriate tests. The question was: what sort of behaviour contributes to the effective performance of the function, and what sort of behavioural tests can assess this type of functional effectiveness?

This development of assessment tools in the field of business management was labelled Assessment Centres, or sometimes Assessment Programmes, since a physical centre was not essential. Although most Assessment Centres used pencil and paper tests, the dominant characteristic was the behavioural test, usually some form of simulation. There has been a great deal of research into the validity of Assessment Centres. One finding was the high level of accuracy in predicting future successful and unsuccessful candidates. The best example was a long-term experiment involving several hundred young people entering the management field of AT & T (American Telephone and Telegraph), and for the purposes of the study the assessors predicted which candidates would and which would not attain middle management level. Unusually, these predictions were kept secret, and concealed from the company. This was to avoid a situation where candidates' career prospects were influenced by the fact that the bosses knew the test scores. Ten years after the predictions, the results were compared with the actual achievements of the candidates. The comparison showed that the tests were remarkably effective in showing in advance those who were likely to succeed in management, and those who were likely to fail. One research worker in the field (Huck, 1977) refers to over fifty studies, all showing positive findings. These findings do not guarantee that the simulation technique will be successful in all circumstances, but it does show that these waters are already well charted. And just as the word 'manager' can be substituted for 'spy', so could the word equally well be 'administrator', 'tutor', 'teacher', or 'student'.

In business management the technique of Assessment Centres has been expensive, but far less expensive than making mistakes when selecting staff for key posts. It is costly because of the quality of the assessors, and also, perhaps, because of the expectations and status of businessmen who utilised the idea. Far less expensive simulation techniques are constantly in operation in business and industry. Selection for all sorts of jobs – airline hostess, policeman, shorthand typist, garage mechanic – often involves a behavioural test in which there is reality of function in a simulated environment.

The following two examples of the simulation technique are taken from the standard procedures of the British Civil Service Selection Board. Both are from the examination for the job of administration trainee (Allen, 1979).

The first is a non-interactive simulation used in the first part of the examination. In this example candidates are asked to imagine that they are administration trainees in the Prime Minister's office. They are asked to write the first draft of a paper listing the points the Government ought to consider as the result of the British invention of a machine by means of which a human being can fly using no power other than that of arms and legs. Details are given about the speed (up to 60 kph), distance of flight (up to 500 km non-stop), size of take-off and landing area (small), and so forth. The candidates are told that they are 'not expected to show any relevant technical knowledge as the draft paper will be considered by technical experts before being submitted to the Cabinet'. But they are encouraged to make recommendations. This is a non-interactive simulation. It is not an exercise or a case study, since the candidates take a specific role, and must write, not as a candidate or as an impartial observer, but as an administration trainee writing a draft document for a British Cabinet.

For those candidates who are successful in the first part of the examination, there is a second stage which includes behavioural interactive simulations. One is known as the 'Committee Exercise'. Each candidate is given specific details of a fairly complex problem and is allowed half an hour to try to grasp what it is all about. The candidates then meet as a committee of six. Each participant takes it in turn to chair the meeting. While in the chair the participants have fifteen minutes in which to present their own particular problem to the committee, analyse the possible solutions, give a lead to the committee, guide the subsequent discussion, and summarise the conclusion. This is something more than an exercise. The candidates have functions, there are plenty of 'facts', and there is a simulated environment. In essence, it is a six-part interactive simulation, with a change of roles every fifteen minutes. It is observed and assessed by members of the staff of the Civil Service Selection Board, and is a standard part of the examination.

Simulations in language examinations

In language teaching, oral language and communication skills are obvious areas for assessment by the simulation technique.

In the chapter on oral language in the Bullock Committee's Report (Bullock, 1975) there is strong criticism of reliance on techniques in which the examiner interviews candidates as a means of assessing oral language. The Report advocates assessment 'in a natural and unforced way'. It quotes from an experiment conducted by the Southern Regional Examination Board in association with the University of Southampton to study the examining on a large scale of oral English, in which 450 candidates were divided into four groups, each of which took a different form of oral examination:

1 reading a passage and talking with the examiner
2 making a short speech or lecture and answering questions
3 talking to the examiner about a diagram previously studied
4 participation in group discussion.

The experimenters concluded that method number 2 was the most 'natural', rewarding and successful; method 3 led to the cultivation of 'civilised conversation', and method 4 measured ability unrevealed in the normal classroom situation. Unfortunately, the research workers had either never heard of the simulation technique, or else assumed that it was part of informal drama. So it was never labelled as a method. However, it seems that methods 2, 3 and 4 all contained simulation elements. And the most successful method – making a short speech or lecture and answering questions – is, or could easily become, a genuine simulation. The examiners' assessment of the four types of oral examination was supported by tape recordings, and by an assessment of the candidates' spoken English by their teachers. The report on the experiment, although expressing conclusions in a tentative way, does state that oral language could be 'sharpened, enriched and disciplined by intelligent and sensitive attention in the classroom and syllabus'.

The use of simulations for assessing oral language and communication skills is likely to be fairer and easier to standardise than the use of informal drama. This conclusion arises out of the nature of the two techniques. In the case of simulations, the data for decision making can be controlled effectively. It is easier to structure a simulation than an informal drama. The motivation in an informal drama might favour good drama at the expense of good argument, and load the dice in favour of the extroverts. This is not to say that informal drama and improvisations can have no place as assessment tools for oral language; but for an examination concerned with assessing the language of function as distinct from the language of the theatre, then simulations are the obvious choice.

In the case of examinations of written language, non-interactive simulations are a possibility and are similar to resource-based questions – questions with maps, graphs, tables of statistics and so on. In Britain, the Schools Council Curriculum Development Project, Geography 16–19, is based on a classroom technique described as the 'Route for Enquiry'. Using such a technique, the teacher rarely stands in front of the class and tells the students what he thinks they ought to know -- except for formal announcements and procedural explanations. The technique is to use simulations, case studies, field-work and exercises. In this project, the Advanced Level syllabus culminates in an external examination, consisting of a three-hour paper of resource-based questions, and also a two-hour paper called a 'decision-making exercise'. In the example given in the pilot study, this 'exercise' was in fact a non-participatory simulation entitled 'More Shops for Abingdon!' The candidate had the role of a planning consultant at a private firm (fictitious) in London, who was asked to recommend one (or perhaps two) of three possible sites for shopping development in Abingdon. The paper contained a great deal of authentic-type material: several maps, a document from Town and Country Property Surveys Ltd, four letters from interested parties, and a brochure about Abingdon.

The key document was a letter to the consultant from the South-West Oxfordshire local authority asking for a balanced assessment of the advantages and disadvantages (economic, environmental and social) of the development of shopping centres at the three proposed sites.

Candidates were told that marks would be allocated to their final report as follows:

	Marks
1 'setting the scene' – an analysis of the background information about the existing situation and Abingdon's future shopping needs	7
2 'identifying the alternatives' – finding out what the possibilities are for future shopping development	8

3 'analysing the alternatives' – considering the impact that
development at each site will make on commerce and business, on the immediate surroundings, and on the lives of
local people   15
4 'weighing up the alternatives' – attempting to balance the
advantages and disadvantages of each site and to make a
final decision   10
5 'recommending and justifying' – recommending where new
development should take place, and providing well-reasoned
justification for this   10
                                                                           ────
                                                                                50
                                                                           ────

The paper had no 'right' answer as such. No one received more marks for
choosing one site rather than another. What mattered was how the decisions
were arrived at.

This assessment by non-interactive simulation is based on the assumption
that the teachers used the 'Route for Enquiry' technique. If students brought
up on a diet of lectures, copying and note-taking had to sit such a paper, then
they could have mental apoplexy.

Since the language classroom is becoming more and more a location for
student participation, talk and decision making, it seems only a matter of time
before written language examinations include non-interactive simulations.
As mentioned in the earlier section on the use of simulations in the syllabus, a
formal classroom assessment of the work done on the course automatically
means that the teaching tools are also the assessing tools. If the language
teacher uses role play, exercises, simulations, informal drama and games,
then the language and behaviour of the students in these activities contribute
to the marks awarded.

By way of comparison, the weighting of the marks awarded by class
teachers in the Schools Council geography project is as follows:

Knowledge (of principles and of specifics)   40%
Skills (intellectual and communication skills,
          including values inquiry and decision making)   40%
Practical skills and techniques   20%

In the Schools Council project, the simulation technique was not regarded as
a sophisticated method suitable only for the advanced students. The same
'Route for Enquiry' method was used with less able students, and the main
conclusion was: 'A wide variety of teaching resources and methods is needed
to stimulate and sustain interest. Audio-visual presentations, simulations and
field-work were most popular.'

The Schools Council geography project seems a good example of the philosophy of 'language across the curriculum' – a phrase given currency as the title of Chapter 12 of the Bullock Report. The phrase refers to the need for teachers of all subjects to be aware of 'the linguistic processes by which their pupils acquire information and understanding'.

Clearly, the language teacher is in a far more favourable position to incorporate the simulation technique into the formal assessment of the students' class work than is the case in many other subject areas. The door is wide open for oral work, and the assessment of oral skills. Nor does the Controller have to be a simulation expert to carry out such assessments. It is not the simulation as such which is being assessed, it is the language skills of the participants.

Informal assessments

In simulations, the interaction is a built-in assessment, informal and personal, by the participants. Interaction would not take place if there were a complete failure to communicate. Unlike an answer in a written examination, and unlike a piece of silent learning, a simulation involves instant feedback. The interaction consists of causes and effects, actions and reactions, questions and answers. If the language of a participant is muddled, inaccurate or ambiguous, then this is likely to be revealed immediately in the responses of the other participants: 'What do you mean?' 'Are you saying that...?' 'Say that again.' Participants continuously assess each other's language, not from the point of view of pedantry, but from the aspect of function and meaning.

Language in a simulation is not theoretical. In a classroom situation the teacher can ask 'Do you all understand this?', and everyone may respond 'Yes, I understand.' But it is one thing to believe that something is understood in theory, and quite another to show that it is understood in practice. A simulation is the practical test, and the assessment of language that goes on during the course of a simulation is substantial in quantity and quality. And this assessment continues along its informal and personal path in retrospect, after the event has ended.

Informal assessments by the Controller are also inevitably and inescapably part of the simulation experience. Consciously or unconsciously the Controller observes a whole range of language and behaviour. This occurs for two main reasons: firstly, the Controller is not involved in the action, and the Controller's main function is that of observer; secondly, the participants' language and behaviour are non-routine and have the virtue of the unexpected, or at least the interesting. The range of possibilities is very great, since the participants own the simulation and shape the event. Thus, a simulation combines the opportunity and the incentive for the Controller to make informal assessments of what is going on. So even if these assessments do not always result in a formal award of marks, they still form the basis of the Controller's judgements about the efficacy of the teaching and the syllabus.

Conclusions and suggestions for assessment

The importance of the question of having simulations in examinations is supported by the weight of evidence of what is being done and what can be done in this field. Assessment in language teaching is not only an area which is ripe for change, it is also within the province of the educational establishment to change it. Examination boards control what is examined. What is examined helps to determine what is taught and how it is taught. The following four suggestions may help to focus attention on the sort of practical measures which examination boards, syllabus designers, tutors and teachers might bear in mind.

1 A gradual movement towards resource-based questions and non-interactive simulations in examinations of written language would have an immediate and beneficial effect on classroom techniques. While it would be unfair on candidates if the external examination techniques were too far ahead of teaching practices, the gradual introduction of such a move, plus publicity given to the move, would reduce or eliminate the danger of unfairness.

2 A study could be made of the types of interactive simulation which are suitable for oral examinations. Probably these would have to be well balanced and reasonably short, with provisions within the mechanics of the simulation for equal opportunities for each participant.

3 Whenever appropriate, syllabuses should be designed to incorporate and encourage participant interaction, simulations, role play and the inquiry technique. Behavioural assessment, including language assessment, by the teacher of these activities should become an important element of the total marks for the course.

In certain circumstances it should be possible to build the course around simulations. Such simulations would then provide points of focus and points of comparison. In such courses, the assessment could take on a developmental aspect, assessing not just one simulation event, but progress through several such events.

4 In the training of language teachers, and in in-service training, there could be greater emphasis on the simulation technique as a tool for assessing teaching ability. This would not only serve to improve ability, but would also result in a greater awareness of what a simulation is, and how it can be used effectively in the language classroom.

8 Simulations in teacher training

Simulations about teaching

Just as teachers are important to simulations, so too can simulations have a beneficial effect on teachers. Experience of the simulation technique should be an essential part of the language teacher's training, including in-service training. There are hundreds of simulations which are suitable for this purpose. Quite a few published simulations deal specifically with the educational scene, and have roles for teachers, students, inspectors and administrators. There are also many unpublished simulations of this nature in current use. The subject matter is as varied as education itself. Some simulations deal with curriculum problems and inter-departmental disputes about the timetable. Others are concerned with the head teacher's in-tray, and with problems involving parents and the local educational authorities. Some simulations are located in the teachers' staff room. Several simulations are about a classroom situation, with roles for the teacher or teachers who are in charge of a particular lesson, and the bulk of the participants function as students. In one way or another, these simulations involve language in an educational context.

The advantages include that of relevance, but there can also be disadvantages of relevance. The situation could be too close to the professional jobs of the participants, who might be reluctant to face the possibility of their professional competence coming under scrutiny and criticism. A head teacher, for example, may object to taking that function in a simulation. If a person is pressurised by the Controller into taking a role too close to their professional job, then the results could be unfortunate. The participant might play it for laughs, in order to put up a decoy target which would deflect personal and professional criticism. In selecting simulations for teacher training it is worth looking for those simulations which contain the essence of the functions but without trying to imitate all the details. In fact, if the educational details are quite different from those that the teachers are used to, then there is less danger of the participants acting and play-acting.

If the Controller is dealing with teachers who have had no experience of simulations, then an overview briefing is particularly important, even more so than in the case of students. There are two main reasons for this, both involving professional experience. Firstly, some of the teachers may well be experienced in using role play or informal drama, and may assume that a simulation is the same thing, but with a few more documents. So they may think that acting is acceptable, and that imaginative creativity of 'facts' is permitted and even to be encouraged. Secondly, personality and professional defensive mechanisms may lead to sabotage. In any random group of people it will not be surprising if several of them are particularly conscious of their own dignity, and seek to avoid situations in which it might be threatened. Without an overview briefing, interspersed with encouraging and reassuring remarks, a few participants might well take defensive measures in a simulation. This could be minimal participation, over-formal participation and non-participation, with the participant not accepting the role, but standing outside the simulation mentally, and criticising it from a teaching point of view while it is going on. Remarks like 'This is kid's stuff', 'I don't want to make a fool of myself', 'I don't know what I'm supposed to do' and 'I can't see the sort of children I have to teach being interested in this' – these are all non-simulation remarks if they occur in the action. They can sabotage a simulation, and may well be intended to do just that – to prevent the other participants also from accepting their roles. The other common form of defensive sabotage among professionals is ham acting. It is likely to occur when a participant is over-sensitive to criticism, and feels insecure among colleagues. So, instead of fulfilling the obligation to behave naturally and accept the role and the function, the participant resorts to caricature and farce.

While an overview can directly, or indirectly, provide reassurances in order to reduce anxiety, there may well be several anxious participants who wish to prolong the briefing in order to delay the simulation, or – better still from their point of view – reduce the amount of time available for it. The sort of things that crop up in such a situation are requests for greater clarification of the aims and principles of the simulation technique, inquiries about the place of the simulation technique in language teaching, and general and specific doubts about the value of simulations. While it may not be possible for the Controller to be sure whether the queries are genuine or merely delaying tactics, it is probable that if two or three potential participants keep making all the objections, then personality issues are involved.

From this somewhat lengthy description of potential personality problems in relation to teachers doing simulations about teachers, it should not be assumed that the area as a whole is dangerous. Most of the teachers in the college or on the course, including the more nervous ones, are likely to accept the basic idea of a 'safe' behavioural situation. Like flying, teaching can be tense and hazardous, and it makes sense to simulate the conditions before the pilot, or teacher, has his first solo. The functions are real, but the consequences of errors and misjudgements do not have disastrous results. Simulations are also an opportunity to experiment a bit, and be a little more daring than might be the case with an over-cautious person in a real environment. For similar reasons, there is likely to be a general intellectual acceptance of the need for the occasional 'disaster' simulation, where lots of things go wrong: the parents are up in arms, the local authorities are looking for scapegoats, and the pupils are misbehaving.

Teaching about simulations

Teacher training provides a particularly suitable opportunity for learning about simulations. The benefits need explaining, and the misunderstandings need to be dispelled. This is true of teacher training in general; it is even more important in the training of language teachers.

Simulations should have a place in teacher training appropriate to the educational importance of the technique. If the teacher training institution does not include any provision in the syllabus for teaching about simulations, but is considering how this might be done in the future, then various options are open, ranging from the timid to the brave. The timid option is to arrange for a half-hour talk on simulations in the second year of the course by a staff member who is assumed to have some knowledge of simulations because of a background of informal drama. The talk can be accompanied by two or three published simulations in package form so that the student teachers can try to appraise the technique by inspecting the materials. The brave option is to structure the course around simulation participation. In addition, various simulation experts can be brought in from other parts of the education field (or even from industry or the armed forces) to demonstrate aspects of the technique.

In choosing the brave option, the course designer could have four main aims in mind. One is the obvious one of allowing the student teachers to learn about simulations from the hot seat – actual participation. Secondly, the experiences would improve their teaching abilities by practising a wide variety of communication skills and functions. Thirdly, the particular simulations would be chosen as relevant to the syllabus, providing points of focus, comparison and incentive. Fourthly, the simulation behaviour of the student teachers would be assessed by the tutors; a behavioural assessment for a behavioural occupation, and an assessment which could take note of behaviour, skills and attitudes which might not otherwise be revealed.

If the syllabus is to be structured around simulations, then it is important to get the words right. An example of how things could go wrong comes from the University of California at Berkeley, where a course on sociology consisted of nothing but simulations. The educational results were excellent, but unfortunately the course had been advertised as being based on 'games', and this attracted unfavourable publicity. There was hostility from parents, politicians and administrators, who objected to the students 'playing games instead of learning'. The course was not repeated.

Apart from learning about simulations, and being assessed by simulations, there is also the option of teachers designing their own simulations. For many years, the University of London Institute of Education has run a curriculum option course entitled 'Games and Simulations in Education'. It is part of the Post Graduate Certificate of Education. Those students who take the course are marked by the tutor's assessment of their work, and this amounts to 25 per cent of the total marks for the whole certificate examination. During the course, the students are expected to devise, write and test a game or simulation in their own subject area, and to produce a 2,000-word report on their efforts – what they did, why they did it, how they altered it, and so on. Even if a student designs a game, not a simulation, the activity of doing so could be regarded as a simulation since the student had the functional role of games designer in a simulated environment. The testing was usually done in schools, so this aspect was not a simulation, as it was a real environment, with real pupils or students. The course includes plenty of experience and participation in games and simulations, and the tutor's assessment is essentially behavioural – observing how the students tackle problems and reach decisions, and how they communicate their ideas, including the merits of the 2,000-word reports.

These examples show that simulations can be given an important place in teacher training. Providing the curriculum designers know the rocks and the main currents, then the inherent advantages of the simulation technique will ensure that the ship reaches harbour.

Appendix A: *We're not going to use simulations*

by Ken Jones

This simulation about simulations may be photocopied by the reader and used for educational purposes. But it must not be distributed outside the school or college, and it must not be sold.

Controller's notes

Introduction

We're not going to use simulations is a simulation by Ken Jones designed for teacher training, particularly for those who have little or no experience of simulations.

It is open-ended, with no 'right' answers, and is fully participatory, with no part-time or passive roles. It gives opportunities for practising language and communication skills, and for dealing with official documents. It usually lasts between 1½ and 3 hours, including briefing and debriefing, and can be used by six to thirty participants.

Scenario

The simulation is about three teachers of English as a foreign language, who have decided to appeal against a Ministry of Education decision that simulations should be used as frequently as possible in all English classes in all schools from the third year upwards. The setting is the Republic of Lingua, and the Appeal is heard by three members of the Inspectorate at Ministry House, Linguan City.

The simulation has two stages – the preliminary discussions and the Appeals hearing. In the first stage, the two sides – the teachers and the inspectors – meet separately and discuss what they should say and who should say it. These meetings are informal, and the relevant documents can be discussed and explored. Since the participants are in teams, this means that any less able student will receive help from the other members of the team in understanding the language and meaning of the documents.

The second stage of the simulation is the Appeals hearing itself. This is formal. Whereas the language used in the first stage is likely to be exploratory and conditional, the language in the second stage is likely to be that of statement and explanation, and of question and answer.

Documents

There are twelve documents in the simulation, as follows:

Notes for participants: This is for all the participants. It explains what the simulation is all about. It is used only during the briefing.

Six individual role cards: These are for the individual participants – for Inspectors Ai, Bee and Cee, and for Teachers Jay, Kay and Ell. They give background information.

Five official documents:
1 Report of the 'Zed Incident'
2 Ministry of Education Decision Paper (page 61)
3 Appeals Procedure (page 14)
4 Application for Appeal from the Head Teacher of Blue School
5 Letter from the Ministry granting permission to appeal

The role cards and the official documents are for use during both the preliminary meetings and the Appeals hearing.

The first step

The best way – and some would say the only way – to know what is involved in a simulation is to participate in it. A simulation is not like a novel or a poem; it cannot be assessed merely by inspecting the materials. Many simulations, including this one, contain deliberate gaps, ambiguities and opportunities which may not be apparent from just reading the documents. For example, none of the role cards point out the ambiguity of the word 'should' in the Ministry's decision that 'Simulations should be used...' Is this advice, exhortation, or an order? Any participant can seize on this point and argue it; and if they do not, the Controller can raise it in the debriefing – and more effectively than if the materials themselves had prompted the participants, since failure is often more important in learning than success. Certainly the Controller should not drop hints beforehand.

A second important advantage of preliminary participation is that the Controller will be better able to assess the level of language difficulty of a simulation. All too often an outsider tends to think the materials and procedures in a simulation are too difficult. This assessment can easily be inaccurate if the Controller has not taken into account the motivation involved, and the interchange of ideas and explanations among the participants themselves.

The first step is for the Controller to gather together a few friends or colleagues for an hour or so, and have a go. It is not necessary to complete the whole simulation, and corners can be cut. But enough time should be allowed to get into the action.

This preliminary excursion into action will also give the Controller an idea of the mechanics of the simulation – timing, briefing, room space, furniture and so on.

Participation also gives the Controller the needed confidence and ability to introduce the simulation effectively and in a relaxed manner.

Numbers and timing

The ideal number of participants is six – one participant for each role card – or multiples of six, with identical materials for each group. If the numbers are not divisible by six, it is possible for participants to share a role, or for one participant to have two role cards.

With large numbers it may be useful to appoint one or two Deputy Controllers, who would assist with the mechanics and perhaps act as observers and monitor the language, communication and decision-making skills.

Timing is also flexible. The simulation can be taken in stages, with gaps for a meal break or coffee break in between some or all of the stages. The two stages of the action part of the simulation could be separated by a break. There could be a break between the briefing and the action, and between the action and the debriefing.

There are advantages in building in a break. It is realistic to assume that there would be a time interval between a preliminary discussion and the hearing itself, and such a built-in break can help add to the realism, especially if this is explained by the Controller in the briefing. If there is a break between the briefing and the action, then this helps the participants to think themselves into the situation.

A gap between the action and the debriefing is useful because it allows the participants time to get over the involvement and tenseness, and to assemble their thoughts.

If a gap is as long as a day, or even several days, then there are dangers of discontinuity. Students can lose a sense of involvement. Some students may turn up in the middle of the simulation, whereas one or two who were present for the part before the break may be missing after it. These problems can be dealt with, but they should be thought about in deciding the timing. If only one or two students are likely to miss part of the simulation, then the problem could be solved by making late comers into observers, and possibly role-sharing to cover absent participants. But if a more substantial number of students were likely to miss part of the simulation, then it would be better to try to complete the action part in one session.

The average time for the whole of the simulation, including briefing and debriefing, is probably between 1 ½ and 3 hours. If both Controller and students are used to situations where the students work independently and in groups, then it is easier for the Controller to make an estimate of the time needed, since there will be no delays caused by the novelty of students being faced with the powers and responsibilities of decision making. Linguistic ability has a double-sided influence on timing. Less able students take longer to read the documents, but spend less time on the action and decision making. The more able the students, the longer the simulation can take.

Furniture and room space

An important consideration is realism. The arrangement of the furniture should be appropriate to the action. If the action is restricted to one classroom with hard chairs and small tables, then there is clearly less scope for touches of realism. But if it is possible for other space to be available – the staff room, the canteen, or even a bench in the college grounds – then such settings would be realistic and appropriate for the first part of the action, the informal (and comfortable) meetings of the two sides separately.

The location for the second part of the action should be chosen to reflect the face-to-face formality of the Appeals hearing. It would be inappropriate for this part of the simulation to be conducted by participants lolling about in comfortable armchairs, or sitting at a coffee table. There should be a table behind which the inspectors sit, and the teachers should sit facing them, perhaps with their own table, on which they can spread the documents and notes they have made. There could be realistic touches, such as a green baize cloth, a carafe of water and glasses, clean note pads and sharpened pencils.

If only one classroom is available, and if there are twelve participants, then the furniture for the briefing, the informal meetings, the hearing and the debriefing could be as follows:

The briefing. In the briefing the students are still students, and are briefed as individuals, and not in groups.

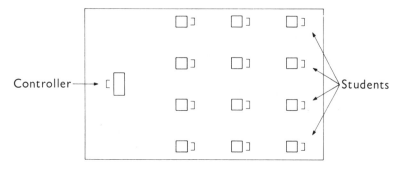

The action – stage 1. The students are now participants and work together to decide what they should say at the Appeals hearing.

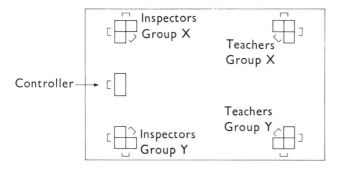

The action – stage 2. The formal Appeals hearing, with the two groups operating simultaneously, but kept as far apart as possible.

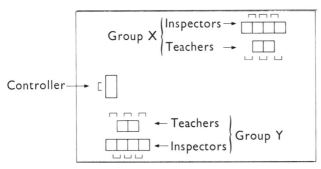

The debriefing. It is useful to retain the groups and the confrontation element, even though the action is over. This helps group consultation, and identification of who is who.

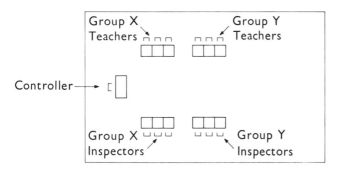

As well as the location of furniture, the Controller can also consider additional items which can add to the realism or the communication facilities. For example, name cards can be useful — perhaps as a piece of folded paper on the desks at the hearing. This helps the participants if they wish to use the names of the people at the meeting, and also to remember who is who afterwards at the debriefing.

The names can be short or long: Cee, or Inspector Cee, or Inspector Anita Cee; and Jay, or Teacher Jay, or Teacher Ahmed Jay.

These materials should be prepared before the briefing if at all possible, and they should be done with a reasonable degree of care, thus reflecting the Controller's view of the importance of the simulation. There can be notices representing place names, 'Inspectors' Lounge, Ministry House' and 'Staff Room, Blue School', to represent suitable locations for the preliminary meetings. If several groups are operating simultaneously, then there could be different notices, colour coded to indicate which group is which.

In preparing these materials, the Controller may wish to consider (invent) some social conventions of Lingua. For example, if the class includes both sexes, then it can be explained that Linguan law forbids sex discrimination in job recruitment, and that Linguan custom allows women equal rights of expression with men. It can be a further Linguan convention that the words 'Mr', 'Miss' and 'Mrs' are not used in conversation, and are replaced by job titles, such as 'Teacher', 'Doctor' and 'Sales Manager'.

No role card involves a sex change, and all role cards allow equal freedom of expression.

The briefing

A briefing in a simulation should be concerned solely with the mechanics — the timing, the location and the allocation of roles, together with a generalised description of what is involved.

In a simulation the participants must have full power and authority to make their own mistakes. Thus, a simulation is like life in the world outside the classroom. The difference is that the Controller can observe what is going on, and the students can learn from their own mistakes in a safe environment. Failures and successes can be explored at the debriefing.

This means that the nature of a simulation involves realism. The participants should be allowed to examine the documents on their own and make their own assessments, explanations and decisions. The Controller should avoid any temptation to help the student by examining the documents in the briefing.

Even if a simulation is being used to help students use English as a foreign or second language, the Controller should try to avoid giving anything more than generalised advice on language in the briefing. This could cover the modes of speech which are likely to arise; whether the language is that of information seeking, of question and answer, or whether it is concerned with exhortation and argument, and so forth. Also, any unfamiliar fact or word can be explained, if this is thought necessary for the smooth running of the simulation. In general, it is better for the Controller to err on the side of explaining too little rather than too much.

The mechanics of the simulation should be explained carefully, since the participants can themselves help to run the simulation if they are aware in advance of how much time is allowed for each part of the simulation, who sits where, and where the furniture should be located.

If the simulation is restricted to one classroom, and if there is more than one group operating simultaneously, it is useful for the Controller to come to the briefing equipped with diagrams showing where the tables and chairs should be located.

The mechanics regarding timing will depend on whether there is an actual deadline for the activity to end – a meal break, or the end of the teaching period – or whether the Controller can extend the activity into a further session. If the total time allowed is inflexible, then it is important in the briefing to set a deadline for the end of the Appeals hearing, so as to allow adequate time for the debriefing session. This is an important point, since there is otherwise a danger of the involvement and motivation being so strong that the action part of the simulation could overrun, with little or no time for debriefing, leaving the students dissatisfied because they never found out about the problems, decisions and role cards of the other participants.

Roles are best allocated at random, which accords with the nature of a simulation. It is fair; it is seen to be fair, and everyone has the same chance. A simulation is not like a play, where people are allocated roles in order to produce the best possible performance. The role cards can be placed face down on the table, and the students can then pick their own cards.

One seeming disadvantage of this advice is that one or two students may know a good deal about simulations already, and yet may find themselves in the role of a teacher with no experience of simulations. Should this occur, then the Controller may wish to ask those individuals to block off their knowledge of simulations, which is not too difficult to do. It does not, for example, involve any acting or personality change. They are teachers in Lingua, and they have had no simulation experience, and that is that.

If the action starts immediately after the briefing, then it is important for the Controller to have made sure that all the documents are available, and in the right order and numbers for handing out: first the notes for participants, then the role cards, and finally, when the participants are in groups, the five official documents. If large numbers of participants are involved, then it is a good idea to select one or two students as Deputy Controllers, perhaps having previously briefed them in the mechanics of the simulation so that they know in advance what they are expected to do.

The action

Providing the Controller has already participated in the simulation, and assuming the briefing was adequate, then the action should run itself. The Controller can relax and observe. A simulation is not taught, and the Controller's job is to see that the simulation flows smoothly.

The Controller, when talking directly to the students between stages, should adopt a tone of deference and respect, as befitting the honourable teachers and inspectors of the Republic of Lingua, and refer to them by their role card names. Thus, the Controller might act as usher to announce the arrival of the three teachers for their meeting with the inspectors.

During the action itself, the Controller should not interfere at all – no little hints, smiles, frowns or other forms of body language. A poker face should be cultivated, which helps to discourage any students from turning to the Controller for advice on policy questions. One technique for observing without interfering – particularly when several groups are operating simultaneously – is to walk around very slowly, looking neither to the left nor right, but at the same time listening to what is being said in the different groups.

Alternatively, the Controller can sit or stand unobtrusively, perhaps taking notes, but avoiding eye contact with the participants.

The debriefing

A useful technique is to start the debriefing with everyone (including the Controller) taking it in turns to explain what special information they had, what their problems were, and how they tackled them. This puts everyone in the picture, as well as providing the raw material for the subsequent discussion. It also gives more practice in communication skills. There should be no discussion or argument during this round-the-class report session; it should be regarded as a series of statements of fact.

The discussion that follows can explore whatever aspects are thought most useful or most interesting. It will probably concentrate on two areas – the language used and the simulation technique.

The simulation will have provided both Controller and students with plenty of examples of the use of English in an informal and a formal situation. The two can be contrasted.

In the informal preliminary discussion the language was concerned with exploration of the situation and with planning. Each group operated as a team with a common purpose. There was probably little in the way of speech making, or of waiting politely for someone else to finish speaking. Interruptions would be fairly common: 'Yes, but...' 'Just a minute' 'No, no' 'That's right, and...' Not much time would elapse between a participant thinking of a point and expressing it.

It might also be worth exploring whether there was any difference between the language and behaviour of the two groups in the informal discussion. Were inspectors slower of speech, and perhaps slightly pompous in the way they explained their points of view? Did the teachers have their heads closer together than the inspectors during the preliminary discussions? Such findings would not be unusual, since the teachers have a common grievance whereas the inspectors have a duty to be reasonably impartial. But whatever the reasons, it affects the language, and this is worth recognising.

During the Appeals hearing itself, the Controller will probably have observed much more than the participants: for example, the approximate number of times the inspectors interrupted the teachers to ask a question or insert an explanation, and whether the teachers ever interrupted the inspectors. What sort of language was used in the interruptions: 'Excuse me' 'With respect, may I...'? Which participants, if any, used people's names, and what effect did this have in the minds of the speaker, the listener, and the other participants? Were any ambivalent expressions used: 'Thank you, Teacher Kay, but...' 'I appreciate that point, Inspector, but...'?

Although the language used by the participants will vary according to ability, maturity and experience, the basic forms are likely to be similar. Thus the observations made by the Controller when trying the simulation for the first time (perhaps with a group of friends or colleagues) will be of considerable help in anticipating, monitoring and assessing what happens on future occasions.

The second major topic of the debriefing – the nature and use of simulations – has two aspects.

One aspect is the common experience of participating in the same simulation. The raw material for discussion is immediate and mutual. Irrespective of the subject matter, the students have taken part in a simulation and experienced some of the problems and opportunities of having the powers, responsibilities and duties which are implicit in all simulations. For those students who have never participated in a genuine simulation the experience is likely to be most valuable – far better than listening to someone describe what a simulation is.

The second aspect is the use of simulations in a wide variety of conditions (including that of using simulations with students in their third year of English). For this discussion on simulations in general far more information is available than could possibly be included on the role cards. These notes, for example, can be used as source material which could be dropped in at various points in the debriefing.

Only two of the six role cards contain any authoritative information about simulations in general – those of Inspectors Bee and Cee – and these contain some significant and deliberate omissions. The reason for this is to give the participants a chance of coming up with their own ideas, rather than trotting out a pat answer.

One deliberate gap is on the question of discipline: what happens if another Zed incident develops with the participants fooling around and playing it for laughs? The nearest to an answer comes in Inspector Bee's role card, which says that the participants must accept their functions, roles, duties and responsibilities, otherwise there is no simulation. The participants must be statesmen, survivors, businessmen and so on, and not comedians or saboteurs or actors.

What the role card could say, but does not say, is that it is important to choose the right simulation in the first place and introduce it effectively, and that if anything seems to be going wrong in the action, then it should be dealt with by the Controller within the context of the activity: an urgent message from the managing director, or whoever is appropriate, asking the offending participant to come for an immediate consultation. By withdrawing the participant from the action the Controller can find out what the matter is. It might be due to a misunderstanding, or the behaviour may have nothing to do with the simulation. The participant could be allowed to continue the simulation in the same role, or change roles, or help the Controller.

Another omission from the role cards is the advantages of the simulation technique in language learning: that it is highly motivational; that it helps confidence; that it enables the Controller to observe the language and behaviour from a neutral position; that it can reveal language and behavioural skills which may not normally arise in the classroom; and that simulations can be used for assessing oral and written language. No role card mentions simulations as icebreakers, or simulations as aids in cross-cultural studies, or in learning languages for specific purposes.

Nor did any role card draw the conclusion that *Walking the Tightrope* was not a simulation. Mrs Zed's classroom activity contained no reality of function, since an audience cannot push a tightrope walker, and the tightrope walker was not, in any case, walking a tightrope, but only mimicking the activity. It might be described as an informal drama, or a confrontational mimicry exercise, but simulation it definitely was not.

The role cards for the inspectors and the teachers are very different. Inspector Ai's card deals with procedure and mentions definitions; the cards for Inspectors Bee and Cee contain little else apart from descriptions of what a simulation is and is not; while the role cards for Teachers Jay, Kay and Ell are almost exclusively devoted to conditions in Blue School, plus some misunderstandings about simulations and about *Walking the Tightrope* in particular. The middle ground is occupied by some rather ambiguously worded official documents. And the problem is what the two sides are going to talk about.

Follow-up activities

We're not going to use simulations is unusual, since the subject matter is the simulation technique itself. The main avenue for follow-up activities would seem to be an exploration of other simulations and how they could be used for learning and also for assessment. The objective might be to get behind the label – business simulations, foreign affairs simulations and so on – and find out what actually happens during the event: what sort of skills are used by the participants, and what are their duties and responsibilities?

One practical activity might be the writing of simulations, and the forming of a guinea pig club to test them.

The exploration could look beyond the educational field into the use of simulations in industry or the armed forces, and experts in these fields might be invited to give a talk or a demonstration of their experiences.

Another follow-up area might be the development of simulations for assessment purposes in both formal examinations and in classroom assessment.

Teachers who may be moving from 'interested' to 'keen' in their attitude to simulations might consider joining a society. The three main societies are the British association, SAGSET (Society for Academic Gaming and Simulation in Education and Training); NASAGA (North American Simulation and Gaming Association); and ISAGA (International Simulation and Gaming Association). Details of these societies, together with references to individual simulations and books about simulations are contained in the bibliography at the end of this book.

Notes for participants

What it's all about

This is a simulation about the simulation technique.

You are either one of three teachers – Jay, Kay or Ell – who are objecting to using simulations for the teaching of English as a foreign language, or you are one of three inspectors – Ai, Bee or Cee – who are to hear the Appeal. The country concerned is the Republic of Lingua.

In the first part of the simulation the two sides meet separately to discuss the situation, and perhaps decide who should say what at the hearing.

The second part of the simulation is the hearing itself.

What you can do, and what you can't do

You cannot invent 'facts' in order to win arguments. The only facts are those contained in the five documents and in the individual role cards.

If your role card says that you have no experience of simulations, then you must not invent any personal knowledge of any simulation in Lingua.

Although 'facts' cannot be invented, opinions and speculation are free, and you can put forward whatever arguments or views seem appropriate to the situation – you are not restricted to putting forward only those opinions which are on your role card. You can also change your mind after hearing the arguments.

You can never step outside the simulation and say 'This is a simulation and this is good (or bad).' As a Linguan you are not taking part in a simulation, you are taking part in an Appeal.

Advice

Read your role card carefully. This is not confidential, and if you wish, you can discuss it with your colleagues.

The five documents are important, since these give details about the background to the Appeal, and the procedure to be followed at the Appeal. There is one document from the Head Teacher asking for the Appeal, and there is a reply to this from the Ministry agreeing to the hearing. The Appeal procedure is contained in the 'Appeals – Ministry of Education' document. The other two documents are a report on the 'Zed Incident' and page 61 of the Ministry of Education Decision Paper, which contains the decision which the three teachers are objecting to.

The Controller is responsible only for the mechanics of the simulation – so do not ask for hints or advice on what you should say at the Appeals hearing.

Role card

Inspector Ai (Chairman)

As Chairman of the Appeal it is my job to see fair play. We must be impartial, and we must be seen to be impartial. Otherwise, there is no point in having an Appeal. I will explain this to Inspector Bee and Inspector Cee before we start. We must not argue with the teachers if we can help it. Our job is to listen carefully, to ask questions, to find out the facts, to explore the situation. This is not a trial, or a confrontation. It is our job to be friendly and sympathetic. I will make this point to the other two inspectors, as they have not sat on an Appeal before.

Although I shall be friendly and helpful, I shall also want to be sure I know the meaning of the words that are used. For example, what do the teachers mean when they use the word 'simulation'? Do they mean the same as the inspectors mean when they say 'simulation'? Does the word mean a package of materials, or does it mean an event in the classroom based on the materials, or does it mean both? I will ask the other inspectors about this before the hearing begins.

The procedure for the Appeal is set out quite clearly in Clause 28 of the 'Appeals – Ministry of Education' document.

But before I ask the appellants to state their case, I shall first welcome them. I will introduce the inspectors and the teachers to each other, and I will ask the teachers if they have copies of the five documents – it is important that each side should have copies of these documents so that they can refer to them at any time they wish.

I shall not make up my own mind about the issue until I have heard what everyone has to say. I hope the hearing will be both pleasant and useful.

Role card

Inspector Bee

This is the first time I have sat on an Appeals hearing. I expect I was chosen because I know quite a lot about simulations.

In Lingua there are now hundreds of published simulations to choose from. They are on all sorts of subjects – business, economics, history, geography, survival, foreign affairs, local government, the environment and so on, and they are all available in English.

The mechanics of the simulations differ widely. Some are short and simple, with only a few documents or even none at all. Others have more documents and can take several hours, several days, or even several weeks to complete.

A simulation is like a case study – a serious study of a problem. But in a simulation the students become participants and get inside the event. They have functions, roles, duties and responsibilities. These must be accepted by the participants, otherwise there is no simulation. The teacher becomes the Controller, responsible for deciding who is who, and who sits where, but with no responsibility for the decision making.

Our experience is that simulations are both useful and popular in language teaching. They provide the students with an opportunity to use language, not for its own sake, but to function effectively.

The document setting out the procedure for this Appeal seems fairly clear; but I will have a word with the Chairman to see whether there is anything else I should know.

Role card

Inspector Cee

I have never taken part in an Appeals hearing. My background is drama and informal drama, and perhaps that is why I was chosen.

A simulation is similar to informal drama, because the students stop being students and take on an identity and have some sort of environment.

But informal drama encourages acting and invention. In a simulation acting is prohibited; what matters is the reality of the function. In a simulation, the chairman of a committee must function conscientiously as a chairman and do the best he can in the situation in which he finds himself. He is the chairman by function. In an informal drama a chairman can imitate the chairman he saw on television the previous night, and invent 'facts' to support the acting. But in a simulation, the basic 'facts' are contained in the background information, and cannot be invented. The chairman is chairman, not an author, or an inventor, or an actor.

Unlike episodic role play, what matters in a simulation is the whole environment, and this is usually structured around some sort of problem which involves all the participants. A simulation can be thought of as reality of function in a simulated and structured environment.

Some simulations are labelled 'games', but this is a mistaken concept. Games have gaming motives. Simulations have functional motives. In games the object is to win. In simulations the object is to function effectively – explaining, deciding, arguing, stating a case – as it is in the world outside the classroom, with duties and responsibilities.

Role card

Teacher Jay

I took over Mrs Zed's class, so I know the conditions and the problems. Like most other classes in the school there are between 25 and 35 students. They are in their third year of learning English. Very few are bright, well-motivated students from the middle and upper classes. Most of them have a working-class background. Some of their fathers are unemployed, and one or two are in prison. When they leave school, most of our students get jobs in factories, or cleaning the streets, or are unemployed.

Our job is to do the best we can to give them an opportunity in life. The important thing is to help them tackle their examinations.

I have had no personal experience of simulation games. Yesterday, when I called for order, one student called out 'Can we play another game – like *Walking the Tightrope?*', and most of the other students laughed.

The problem with classes like these is to find enough time to cover the basic course. There is no time for optional extras, particularly fun and games. Our job is not only to teach language, it is also to see that there are suitable conditions for learning the language. Another Zed incident is the last thing we want.

© Ken Jones 1982

Role card

Teacher Kay

The facts, as I see them, are these: in a simulation game the teacher has no control over the students; they 'own' the simulation. There are two sorts of simulation. There is the behavioural sort, which is what Mrs Zed tried out, and there is the academic sort with lots of facts, figures and bits of paper, as in a business game.

Neither sort of simulation game is suitable for our students and our conditions; the first is too dangerous, and the second is too difficult.

It is not just a question of teaching a language. We have to take into account the ability of the students and also what the students and their parents expect. They expect that such a serious and important subject as language learning will be treated seriously. They understand the importance of education. If we introduce games – or even what they think are games – then we lose their respect.

I have had no personal experience of using simulations. I have nothing against the simulation technique as such; it probably works well in some circumstances, but not with our students.

Role card

Teacher Ell

Like my colleagues, I have had no personal experience of simulations. This is a point of danger in our Appeal. If we are not careful, the inspectors will say, 'All you need is a bit of practice in simulations and then you can start using the technique.' They will then report that the whole problem can be solved with a bit of teacher training.

Even if we were simulation experts, it would not solve our problems. Our main problem is that the general ability of our students is lower and their home background is much worse than in most schools. This means that if we are to do our duty as teachers, we cannot afford to waste time on non-essentials. A good examination result is tremendously important to these students' futures. It makes sense that we should concentrate our teaching efforts on the essentials.

The Zed incident damaged the school in the eyes of the parents. What damages a school also damages the Ministry, and might even damage the Government.

Blue School

Linguan City North
Tel: (0123) 98765

Inspectorate Department,
Ministry of Education,
Ministry House,
Linguan City.

28th January

Application for Appeal

As Head Teacher of Blue School I submit an application for an Appeal against a Ministerial Decision.

The Appeal is against the last sentence of article 163 (page 61) under the heading "Educational Techniques", which reads as follows:

"SIMULATIONS SHOULD BE USED AS FREQUENTLY AS POSSIBLE IN ALL ENGLISH CLASSES FROM THE 3rd YEAR OF ENGLISH TEACHING ONWARDS."

The persons making the Appeal are Teachers Jay, Kay and Ell at Blue School.

Their main argument would be that the simulation technique is not suitable for their classes.

Under Clause 25(b) of the "Appeals - Ministry of Education" document, I give my approval to the Appeal. I do so for three reasons:

(a) I believe the Appeal concerns an important issue

(b) the "Zed Incident" harmed good relations among teachers, students and parents

(c) an Appeals hearing may help to remove any misunderstandings.

T. Kew

Head Teacher
Blue School

MINISTRY OF EDUCATION
Ministry House, Linguan City
Telephone: (0123) 45678

DEPARTMENT OF APPEAL

Head Teacher,
Blue School,
Linguan City North.

Your reference

Our reference 3012/RE

Date 10th February

Dear Head Teacher,

The Inspectorate Department has passed on to us your Application for Appeal against a Ministerial Decision - namely the last sentence of Article 163 (Page 61) of the Ministry of Education Decision Paper.

The Department of Appeal has decided to allow the Appeal to take place, since the application conforms to Clause 25 (b) of the Appeals Procedure.

The hearing will take place in Room 416 at the above address on 1st March at 13.30.

Under the provisions of Clause 27 of the Appeals Procedure, you are hereby instructed to provide your teachers Jay, Kay and Ell, with the documents relating to this case immediately.

The documents are this letter, together with

1.   page 61 of the Ministry of Education Decision Paper

2.   the "Zed Incident" report by Assistant Inspector Dee

3.   page 14 of the "Appeals - Ministry of Education" document

4.   your letter asking for an Appeal.

Please point out to the three teachers that the "Zed Incident" report is private and confidential, and must not be revealed to anyone who is not connected with the hearing of the Appeal.

R. Ess.

Appeals Administrator

MINISTRY OF EDUCATION
Ministry House
Linguan City

The "Zed Incident"

To whom it may concern:

I was requested by both the Inspectorate and the Head Teacher of Blue School to investigate the so-called "Zed Incident". My report is based on an interview with Mrs Zed in hospital, and with 10 students (chosen at random), who were in Mrs Zed's class at the time the incident took place. Although witnesses differed in respect of some details of the incident, there was general agreement that what happened was as follows:

Mrs Zed told the class of about 35 students (in their 3rd year of learning English) that she had invented a simulation which would give them practice and confidence in using English. She described it as "a game called 'Walking the Tightrope'". Mrs Zed explained to the class that in a simulation the students are responsible for their own behaviour; they had a job to do; and she said the teacher (herself) would not interfere. (One or two of the students said they were amazed and delighted to hear this.)

Mrs Zed then drew a chalk line down the centre of the room to represent the tightrope. The class was divided into two groups, called the Red Group and the Blue Group, one at each side of the "tightrope".

In order to play the game, one person from each group had to take it in turn to "walk the tightrope" - that is, walk down the chalk line as if it were a tightrope in a circus. The group to which the tightrope walker belonged had to say words of encouragement. Mrs Zed said she gave as examples - "Well done", "Good work" and "Keep it up". The opposing group, on the other hand, were expected to utter words of discouragement, like "It is dangerous", "You might fall" and "Go back".

Mrs Zed then stood at the back of the room and watched what happened. The result was a rapid escalation into violence and absurdity. Talk became shouting, shouts became insults, insults became threats, and threats became physical attack. At this point Mrs Zed intervened with only partial success to try to separate the two groups, who were fighting each other.

The noise brought the Head Teacher to the scene and order was restored. Mrs Zed was taken home in a shocked condition, and the next day went to hospital where she is under observation.

The class was taken over by Teacher Jay. There were no further attempts at simulations, and behaviour has been excellent.

Assistant Inspector Dee
17th January

APPEALS - MINISTRY OF EDUCATION

23.   All appeals shall be heard at Ministry House, or some other convenient centre, at a time to be determined by the Inspectors.

MINISTERIAL DECISIONS

24.   All Ministerial decisions on educational policy may be subject to appeal.

25.   An appeal may be made by:
(a) a head teacher, or educationalist of equal status or above, or
(b) by at least two classroom teachers, provided that the appeal has the approval of the head teacher concerned.

26.   An appeal is heard by three members of the Inspectorate.

27.   All documents related to the hearing must be exchanged between the two sides at least one week before the date of the hearing.

28.   An appeal has 4 main sections:
(a) the appellants state their case (each appellant should speak)
(b) the Inspectors may then question the appellants
(c) the Inspectors give opinions (each Inspector should speak)
(d) the two sides may then exchange further views.

29.   Immediately after the final exchange of views, the Inspectors may give an immediate decision, or defer a decision for further consideration.

30.   The Inspectors are permitted to interpret Ministerial decisions, but have no power to change Ministerial decisions.

31.   The Inspectors are empowered to recommend changes, additions, or deletions concerning Ministerial decisions. Such recommendations will be considered at Ministerial level.

DEPARTMENTAL DECISIONS

32.   Departmental decisions include all decisions taken by officials at

© Ken Jones 1982

that a new teacher training college will open next year. These decisions reflect the Ministry's view that teacher training is of fundamental importance.

PART 3   EDUCATIONAL TECHNIQUES

SIMULATION

161.   Although simulation is a relatively new technique in Linguan education, it is a valuable educational tool in some learning situations.

162.   All students at teacher training colleges must participate in at least one simulation each term.

163.   In the learning of the English language, the simulation technique was tested in an experiment at Ministry House College involving 73 intermediate and advanced students. The results proved that simulations were educationally beneficial and were also popular with the students. Simulations should be used as frequently as possible in all English classes from the 3rd year of English teaching onwards.

TUTORIALS

164.   The tutorial technique has been the subject of much debate at Linguan universities and in higher education generally. Shortage of teaching staff has led to some abuses of the system. In the future, the number of students attending any tutorial must not be larger than three.

165.   The Ministry is preparing a Tutor's Guide to Tutorials which

Appendix B: Eight key reminders

The following eight pages of *Key reminders* are intended as an aid to the language teacher (tutor, or course designer) in explaining aspects of simulations to students, colleagues, administrators and parents.

Although they follow the eight chapter headings, they are not so much summaries as memory triggers – a means of recalling essential points.

They are grouped together rather than added at the end of each chapter in order to provide an overall picture of the book, and also an easily located appendix which can be turned to for instant reference when the need arises, which might occur without warning.

The use of the *Key reminders* requires the reading of the book; they are not a substitute for it. They are a handy source for instant reference, and an insurance against forgetfulness and the subsequent regret – 'What a pity I forgot to make that point.'

The eight titles are:

1 Why use simulations?
2 Choosing simulations for the language classroom
3 Preparing for the simulation
4 The simulation in action
5 The follow-up
6 Will the simulation work?
7 Assessing the result
8 Simulations in teacher training

1 Why use simulations?

A simulation is an event. Although 'simulation' can also be used to describe the package of materials, this meaning is justified by custom, not by accuracy.

A simulation can be defined as 'reality of function in a simulated and structured environment'.

Acting is prohibited. In order for a simulation to occur the participants must accept the duties and responsibilities of their roles and functions, and do the best they can in the situation in which they find themselves.

A simulation is not taught, and the teacher becomes the Controller, and controls the event in the same way as a traffic controller, helping the flow of traffic and avoiding bottlenecks, but not telling individuals which way to go. In the decision-making area the participants 'own' the simulation. It is an event; they are inside the event; they shape the event.

A simulation is not a case study, or an exercise, or a game, or an informal drama, or a bit of episodic role play.

Simulations are both popular and effective in the language classroom because they:
1 remove the teacher, who as Controller, is in an ideal position to monitor the language and behaviour
2 provide realism of both action and (usually) documentation
3 contain built-in motivation, and language which is cohesive in action, focussing on points of duty and function
4 help break the ice and can be used for cross-cultural purposes
5 are an excellent means of assessing language ability.

2 Choosing simulations for the language classroom

In choosing simulations for general language use, interaction is likely to be more important than the subject matter.

It is important to cast a wide net, and to look for simulations which are well designed, provocative, stimulating, consistent and fully participatory, with no passive roles and preferably no part-time roles.

The procedure should include the following steps:
1 Decide on the priority of aims — icebreakers, assessment and so on.
2 Estimate the interactive language competence of the students.
3 Search in a wide area, including simulation literature.
4 If the language level is suitable, then examine the mechanics of the simulation: time, numbers, hardware, space, organisation and so on.
5 If it seems suitable, then participate in it personally.
6 Consider whether it needs adapting, but bear in mind that over-adaptation can kill a good simulation by removing or altering elements which help the simulation to run smoothly in practice.

In general, the second simulation is easier to choose and to run than the first one.

Within the curriculum it is preferable to use several simulations rather than just one.

It is a good idea to try to build the curriculum around simulations rather than try to fit them in as an afterthought.

3 Preparing for the simulation

The first vital step is for the teacher to participate in the simulation personally, since the experience will be invaluable in the briefing and the action, and in the debriefing afterwards.

With students who are new to the simulation technique, an overview briefing about simulations in general will remove misunderstanding and avoid false expectations and inappropriate behaviour.

If in doubt, do not give a language briefing, but concentrate on explaining the mechanics of the simulation — who is who, and who sits where.

Roles should be allocated at random; any key role could be filled by two participants.

If the simulation has several stages, then the Controller should consider giving a small briefing before each stage rather than rely entirely on a main briefing at the start of the simulation.

If the simulation involves formal procedures — such as a parliament or a committee — then the essential rules concerning the procedures for speaking and voting and decision making should be discussed with the students and decided upon before the action starts.

It is absolutely essential to make quite sure that all the necessary documents are available before the simulation begins.

4 The simulation in action

A well-chosen and well-briefed simulation virtually runs itself. The Controller can relax and enjoy the action, while at the same time learning a great deal about the language, social and behavioural skills of the participants.

It is vitally important not to interfere in the decision making, even indirectly by smiles, frowns or small gestures which the participants may look for. The participants must be made to realise that they are on their own, so the Controller's main function during the action is to be as inconspicuous as possible. If movement is necessary in order to monitor the language of different groups, then the Controller should move slowly and not attract attention.

The Controller is fully responsible for the mechanics of the simulation – who sits where, time limits, handing out documents, and so on. This includes responsibility for ensuring that the participants accept their functions. If a participant starts acting around or playing it for laughs, then he has abandoned his function to become a clown or saboteur, and has sacked himself. It is up to the Controller to take him on one side and find out what the matter is, and this should be done within the context of the simulation itself.

Monitoring the language is a matter for professional judgement. The Controller can look for specific language points, or else note points of interest as they arise. Inevitably, the observations will include the monitoring of social, communicative and organisational skills of individual participants and the group as a whole.

5 The follow-up

Probably the best way to start the debriefing is to allow all the participants to take it in turns to say a few words about what their problems were and how they tackled them. This is a continuation of the practice of language and communication skills; it provides an overall picture of the event; and it retains the emphasis on participant involvement.

The debriefing should not be a rerun of the arguments used in the simulation; the discussion can make progress by examining similar and dissimilar situations in the world outside the classroom.

The teacher can guide the debriefing into a consideration of the behaviour in the simulation, or the language, or both. While the participants may welcome comments on the language, it is best to avoid using the debriefing to produce a long list of mistakes. A more positive approach is to use the knowledge gained through the monitoring of the language to help the students at various points during the course.

An analysis of the discourse in the simulation made at leisure from a recording (or the transcript of a recording) can be extremely valuable, from the point of view of grammar and also functional effectiveness.

It is a good idea to have a flexible time period immediately after a simulation in order to be able to take advantage of the students' own ideas and suggestions arising out of the simulation experience.

6 Will the simulation work?

It is valuable to be able to recognise various types and categories of simulation. This helps the teacher to judge and compare simulations, to see whether they fit in with the aims of the course, and whether they are likely to work well or badly in the classroom.

Categorising by subject has limited value for the language teacher, except when language is being taught for a specific purpose. But even here it is important to look behind the label and see what may happen during the event itself.

Some simulations are open-ended, with no 'right' answers. In general, these encourage a wide range of language skills. Closed simulations, with a 'right' answer, usually concentrate the language on a narrower range of options, mainly analytical language.

For general language purposes it is essential to consider the level of interaction. Are there part-time or passive roles, or is the simulation fully participatory? Is the interaction between groups, or between individuals?

Inconsistencies can make a simulation into an unsatisfactory mishmash. It is useful to make sure that there are no unnecessary gaming elements, or invitations to play-act.

A dull, routine simulation can work well enough in the classroom, but have little else to offer. A mind-jogging simulation can not only be fascinating in its operations, but can also produce a lively debriefing and inspire the students in various follow-up activities.

7 Assessing the result

The tools of the assessment should be appropriate to the aims of the assessor. If the aims are behavioural, then the tools should be behavioural.

Experience in many fields, including industry and the armed forces, has shown that simulations are excellent for assessing oral and written language, social and communicative skills, and organisational ability.

In the formal examination of oral skills, the simulation technique is more natural than the interview technique, and is fairer and easier to standardise than the informal drama technique.

In the formal examination of written language, non-interactive simulations can be used, which place the student in a role, with duties and responsibilities for tackling a problem from a particular viewpoint, and with enough information provided about the problem to constitute a structured environment.

If a teacher's assessment of class work is part of the formal marks for the course, then whatever teaching tools are used – role play, projects, simulations – are also the form of the assessment.

Assessment, whether formal or informal, is assisted by the simulation technique because it is natural; it links the classroom to life in the world outside, and it provides opportunities for observing behaviour and language skills which might otherwise not occur in the classroom.

Examination boards should consider the use of simulations in formal examinations; course designers should consider building courses around simulations to help assessment as well as learning.

8 Simulations in teacher training

Some simulations are about teaching. The environment is the staff room, the classroom, or the administration offices, and the participants have appropriate roles and functions to deal with the educational problems. Simulations represent a safe and practical way of learning about the job.

Teaching student teachers about simulations can be done in various ways – from the timid lecture to the bold structuring of the course around simulations. The bold approach has the advantages of placing the student teachers in the hot seat, and learning through participation; it improves their teaching abilities through practice of a variety of communication skills; it provides points of focus, comparison and incentive in the course if suitable simulations are chosen; and it enables the tutor to assess the sorts of behaviour and communication skills of the student teachers which might not otherwise occur during the course.

Another option is to introduce a course which includes practical work of designing simulations (and games), and this can include a written report by individual students on the why and how of simulation design; how they tested the simulation, and how they altered it and improved it.

Simulations should have a place in teacher training according to their educational value, and this particularly applies to the training of language teachers.

Bibliography

Allen, F.H. (1979). Report of the Committee on the *Selection Procedure for the Recruitment of Administration Trainees* under the chairmanship of Dr F.H. Allen. Civil Service Commission, HMSO, London.

Bafá Bafá (1977). Shirts, R.G. Simile II, Del Mar, California.

Barnes, D. *et al.* (1971). *Language, the Learner, and the School.* Penguin Education, Harmondsworth. (This includes the reproduction of the discussion document 'A language policy across the curriculum' by the London Association for the Teaching of English.)

Boocock, S.S. and Schild, E.O. (eds.) (1968). *Simulation Games in Learning.* Sage Publications, Beverly Hills, California.

Bullock, A. (1975). *A Language for Life.* Report of the Committee of Inquiry appointed by the Secretary of State for Education and Science under the chairmanship of Sir Alan Bullock. HMSO, London.

Coulthard, M. (1977). *An Introduction to Discourse Analysis.* Longman, London.

Crisis (c. 1966). Developed by Western Behavioral Sciences Institute. Simile II, Del Mar, California.

Five simple business games (1978). Townsend, C. CRAC/Hobsons Press, Cambridge.

Gibbs, G.I. (ed.) (1974). *Handbook of Games and Simulation Exercises.* E. and F.N. Spon, London, and Sage Publications, Beverly Hills, California.

Halliday, M.A.K. (1978). *Language as Social Semiotic.* Edward Arnold, London.

Horn, R.E. and Cleaves, A. (eds.) (1980). *Guide to Simulations/Games for Education and Training.* 4th edition. Sage Publications, Beverly Hills, California.

Huck, J.R. (1977). The research base. In *Applying the Assessment Center Method.* Moses, J.L. and Byham, W.C. (eds.) Pergamon Press, Oxford.

Humanus. Twelker, P.A. and Layden, K. Simile II, Del Mar, California.

Jones, K. (1974). *Nine Graded Simulations.* (*Survival, Front Page, Radio Covingham, Property Trial, Appointments Board, The Dolphin Project, Airport Controversy, The Azim Crisis, Action for Libel.*) First published by the Inner London Education Authority; now to be published by Max Hueber Verlag, West Germany,1982/3.

Jones, K. (1979). *Space Crash, Outerworld Trade, Rock Island Transport, Is God There?* Management Games, Bedford.

Jones, K. (1980). *Simulations: A Handbook for Teachers.* Kogan Page, London, and Nichols, New York.

Jones, L. (1983). *Eight Simulations.* Cambridge University Press.

Kerr, J.Y.K. (1977). Games and simulations in English language teaching. In *Games, Simulations and Role-playing.* The British Council, London.

Littlewood, W. (1981). *Communicative Language Teaching: An Introduction.* Cambridge University Press.

Man and his Environment (1971). UK. Coca Cola Export Corporation, London.

Megarry, J. (ed.) (1977). *Aspects of Simulation and Gaming.* Anthology of *SAGSET Journal.* Kogan Page, London.

Moses, J.L. (1977). The assessment center method. In *Applying the Assessment Center Method*. Moses, J.L. and Byham, W.C. (eds.) Pergamon Press, Oxford.
North Sea Challenge (1979). Lynch, M. BP Educational Service, London.
OSS (1948). *Assessment of Men*. Selection of personnel for the Office of Strategic Services. Rinehart, New York.
Radio Covingham (1974). Jones, K. First published by the Inner London Education Authority; now to be published by Max Hueber Verlag, West Germany, 1982.
Sinclair, J. and Coulthard, R. (1975). *Towards an Analysis of Discourse*. Oxford University Press.
Space Crash (1979). Jones, K. Management Games, Bedford.
Stadsklev, R. (ed.) (1975). *Handbook of Simulation Gaming in Social Education*. (Part 2. Directory.) Institute of Higher Education Research and Services, the University of Alabama.
Starpower (1969). Shirts, R.G. Simile II, Del Mar, California.
Talking Rocks (1978). Vernon, R.F. Simile II, Del Mar, California.
Taylor, J.L. and Walford, R. (1978). *Learning and the Simulation Game*. Open University Press, Milton Keynes.

Journals and societies

SAGSET (Society for Academic Gaming and Simulation in Education and Training) is the leading European society devoted to the support and encouragement of those who use simulations and games in education and training. Details from: The Secretary, SAGSET, Centre for Extension Studies, University of Technology, Loughborough, Leics. LE11 3TU. The proceedings of the SAGSET conferences have been published yearly since 1975 under the title *Perspectives on Academic Gaming and Simulations*. Kogan Page, London.
Simulation/Games for Learning (formerly *SAGSET Journal*). Quarterly.

NASAGA (North American Simulation and Gaming Association). R.W.T. Nichols, Treasurer, NASAGA, Box 100, Westminster College, New Wilmington, Pa 16142.
Simages. The journal of *NASAGA*.

ISAGA (International Simulation and Gaming Association). It produces a Newsletter available from Dr Jan Klabbers, University of Nijmegen, Department of Psychology, Social Systems Research Group, PO Box 9104, 6500 HE Nijmegen, The Netherlands.

Journal of Experiential Learning and Simulation. Elsevier North Holland Inc, 52 Vanderbilt Avenue, New York, NY 10017.

Simgames. A Canadian quarterly. Champlain Regional College, Lennoxville Campus, Lennoxville, Quebec, Canada, J1M 2A1.

Simulations and Games. An international journal of theory, design and research. Sage Publications, Beverly Hills, California.